John Sayles

Contemporary Film Directors

Edited by James Naremore

The Contemporary Film Directors series provides concise, well-written introductions to directors from around the world and from every level of the film industry. Its chief aims are to broaden our awareness of important artists, to give serious critical attention to their work, and to illustrate the variety and vitality of contemporary cinema. Contributors to the series include an array of internationally respected critics and academics. Each volume contains an incisive critical commentary, an informative interview with the director, and a detailed filmography.

A list of books in the series appears at the end of this book.

John Sayles

David R. Shumway

UNIVERSITY
OF
ILLINOIS
PRESS
URBANA,
CHICAGO,
AND
SPRINGFIELD

Manufactured in the United States of America
1 2 3 4 5 C P 5 4 3 2 1
∞ This book is printed on acid-free paper.

Library of Congress Cataloging-in-Publication Data
Shumway, David R.
John Sayles / David R. Shumway.
p. cm. — (Contemporary film directors)
Includes bibliographical references and index.
Includes filmography.
ISBN 978-0-252-03698-9 (cloth)
ISBN 978-0-252-07856-9 (pbk.)
1. Sayles, John—Criticism and interpretation.
I. Title.
PN1998.3.S3S58 2012
791.4302'33092—dc23 [B] 2011042991

For Travis and Heather

Contents

Acknowledgments

I am grateful to Jim Naremore for asking me to write this book, and for his patience in waiting for it. Lucy Fischer provided an insightful reading of the manuscript and great suggestions for its improvement. Members of the Faculty of Research Colloquium of the Humanities Center at Carnegie Mellon University gave me excellent feedback on Sayles and realism. Joe Skerrett's invitation to a Sayles Symposium at the University of Massachusetts, Amherst, gave me the opportunity to discuss my ideas with a small group of scholars familiar with Sayles's films. I owe thanks to my many research assistants, especially Karensa Cadenas and Michael Lucas. I am most grateful to Heather Arnet, who provided encouragement, intelligent conversation, and a careful reading of most of the book, which I dedicate to her and our wonderful son, Travis.

John Sayles

John Sayles | Critical Realist

John Sayles: Independent

The one word most often associated with John Sayles is *independent*. He has been throughout most of his career referred to as America's leading independent filmmaker. More recently, he has been called both the grandfather and the godfather of American independent cinema. He may be the only filmmaker in the world whose face appears on a seal or medallion. This medallion graces the first page of johnsayles.com, and has appeared after the credits of some of his films. It shows a drawing of Sayles's face, with a legend imprinted around the outside: at the top, "John Sayles," and at the bottom, "Independent" (see figure 1). This designation describes Sayles's relationship to the film industry accurately. He has made only one film within the traditional Hollywood system, where the studio, rather than the director, retains control over casting and cutting.

Figure 1. A symbol of independence: the John Sayles Medallion, from johnsayles.com.

Sayles's own definition of independence is not, however, focused on the relationship of a film to the industry:

> No matter how it's financed, no matter how high or low the budget, for me an independent film emerges when filmmakers started out with a story they wanted to tell and found a way to make that story. If they ended up doing it in the studio system and it's the story they wanted to tell, that's fine. If they ended up getting their money from independent sources, if they ended up using their mother's credit cards, that doesn't matter. (Carson, "Independent" 129).

Sayles therefore considers Martin Scorcese, Spike Lee, Oliver Stone, and Tim Burton independents despite the fact that they have all made movies within the studio system (Smith 250–51). Like them, Sayles has consistently found ways to make the stories he wants to make, though one might add that because of those stories, he has a greater struggle to make them.

Yet, there is something also misleading about the way in which "independent" seems to have become almost a part of Sayles's name. Sayles no more makes films by himself than did Howard Hawks or John Ford.

Indeed, there is no director more conscious of the fact that film is a collaborative medium. In discussing his work in interviews, he always speaks of "our film," not "my film." Those who have worked with him describe the relations on a shoot, not as a hierarchy, but as a community, where the various participants are treated in an egalitarian manner. The image of rugged individualism, which the "independent" label seems to carry, is antithetical to Sayles's practice and to his vision.

Sayles's association with independent cinema also accurately reflects his pioneering role in a movement that developed beginning around 1980 and that might be said to have recently come to an end. As Yannis Tzioumakis has shown, there has always been an independent film sector, in which he includes, for example, producer David O. Selznick in the late 1930s and early 1940s, the production company Walt Disney Pictures in the 1930s, and United Artists as a distributor of independent films from its inception in 1920 until it was sold to a conglomerate in 1967. In the 1960s, major hits like *The Graduate* (Mike Nichols, 1967) and *Easy Rider* (Dennis Hopper, 1969) were produced by entities other than the major studios. But the meaning of the term "independent" had shifted by the end of the 1970s, in part because the industry had consolidated, with film production now controlled by a handful of conglomerates—and in part because of production trends within these companies that focused on making megaprofits on blockbusters like *Jaws* (Steven Spielberg, 1975) and *Star Wars* (George Lucas, 1977). Film had long been an industrial commodity, and during the 1970s, it seemed to become all the more so. But even as the average cost of a Hollywood film was increasing exponentially, the amount of money required to make a movie was actually declining as equipment became less expensive and more readily available.

While avant-garde filmmakers such as Stan Brackage and Jonas Mekas had long made films without the benefit of a production company, very few narrative films were made that way. Sayles's most significant predecessor was John Cassavetes, who beginning with *Shadows* in 1959, wrote, directed, and sometimes edited low-budget and aesthetically innovative films funded by the money he made acting in studio productions. In 1974, he set up his own distribution company, Faces International, to distribute *A Woman under the Influence* when he could not find another company willing to take on the film. Cassavetes's commitment to his own vision was a model for many of the auteurs of 1970s, such as Martin Scorcese, and Sayles has called him a major influence.

When Sayles made his first film, *Return of the Secaucus Seven*, he has said that there were four companies that were in the business of distributing films made outside of mainstream Hollywood (quoted in Anderson). Getting an independent film distributed to theaters was so unusual that Sayles thought his film's best chance to be seen was probably on Public Television, and he consciously shot the film with the small screen in mind. The film's surprising success at the box office and enthusiastic critical reception demonstrated the viability of this new mode of filmmaking. New distributors emerged to handle an increasing number of films made outside of the industry. These films often produced a good return on their small investments, and were thus attractive from a business perspective. The trend culminated in the transformative success of *sex, lies, and videotape* (Steven Soderbergh, 1989), which a small independent company called Miramax acquired after its screening at the Sundance Film Festival. The film's $24 million gross on a $1.2 million cost made independent film something the studios wanted, and they created or acquired divisions to distribute and eventually produce them—rendering, of course, the economic meaning of "independent" moot.

Because Sayles has been defined by his position outside of the industry, in what follows I am attentive to issues of finance and distribution. Although a study of a director who has not been so defined might reasonably ignore his or her position in the market, one cannot deal with Sayles accurately without considering his struggles with financing and distributing his work. I therefore discuss the financing, distribution, and reception of Sayles's films, using the best information available. The point of this is certainly not to buy into the current obsession with box-office performance as a measure of a film's worth, but to make clear the conditions under which Sayles's films have been produced and exhibited, conditions which have affected the way in which these films have been understood and appreciated.

During the 1980s, however, another meaning of the term "independent" emerged that was rooted in "the kinds of formal/aesthetic strategies they adopt" rather than economics and their relationship to the broader social, cultural, political or ideological landscape (King 2).

For some scholars, formal considerations seem to be most important. So, when Juan Suárez observes, "[Jim] Jarmusch has often been regarded as the main exponent of independent cinema in the 1980s and 1990s," it is clearly because of the innovative form his films display (6). Suárez points out that the influence of Jarmusch's films can be seen in the work of Hal Hartley, Sofia Coppola, and Richard Linklater, among others, while Sayles, though often cited as an inspiration by other aspiring filmmakers, does not seem to have been much copied. Others identified as leading independents, including Todd Haynes, Kevin Smith, Gus Van Sant, and Soderbergh, exemplify the sense of "independent" as a filmmaker who experiments with narrative, visual form, or genre, regardless of how the film is financed.

Sayles's critical stance toward American society and its politics is the defining characteristic of his cinema, but that stance has not been expressed through the stylistic experimentation often thought to be required for it. Radical politics are attributed to Jarmusch and Haynes in part because of their style. Sayles has said, "I'm totally uninterested in form for its own sake. But I am interested in story-telling technique" (Smith 100). That distinction is reinforced by his way of discussing his own films in interviews and DVD commentaries, where his concern is mainly how the story got told. He thinks of himself as an artisan or craftsperson, but not as an artist or the maker of "art films." In this sense, Sayles has much in common with studio era directors such as Howard Hawks, who also conceived of themselves as craftsmen and storytellers.

In answering a question about style posed by interviewer Gavin Smith, Sayles offered a longish discussion of Tom Wolfe, Gay Talese, and the new journalism, where he asserted, "I was never interested in it, because I felt that the article wasn't about this actor or this singer or this politician. The article was about Tom Wolfe, about Gay Talese" (101). This suggests that Sayles wants his audience not to be thinking about him, but about the events and characters he is presenting. The answer also implies that Sayles feels a kinship with traditional journalists who give you the story, not their own personalities. Sayles's visual style, then, is always at the service of his story, and he is on occasion visually inventive when the story demands it. He is much more innovative in his narrative structures, which often deviate from standard Hollywood formulas. Yet because "independent" cinema since Cassavetes has been associated with style rather than story, Sayles may be subject to expectations he has no desire to fulfill.

John Sayles: Realist

When Sayles is called a realist in the press, it is usually expressed as the *Los Angeles Times* did in 1995, calling him a "master of gritty realism and champion of the American working class" (Black in Carson, *Interviews* 171). *Realism* here means a particular kind of content, and that content is connected to a traditionally leftist position of support for workers. These are both aspects of Sayles's realism, but many of his films are neither gritty nor are focused on a particular class. Sayles's realism is much broader, including his focus on story and character and his commitment to the idea that film can tell us something about the world out of cinema. Sayles has said, "I always want people to leave the theater thinking about their own lives, not about other movies" (Vecsey in Carson, *Interviews* 96). The desire to make films that make people think about their own lives gets at the essence of the director's realism. What Sayles says he learned from Cassavetes's films was "that you could have recognizable human behavior on the screen" (Smith 51). Whereas film theory and at least some film practice have since the 1970s called into question is the whole idea of realism in cinema, Sayles has never wavered from his ambition to tell us the truth about the world beyond the screen using various means available to the makers of fictions. In arguing that Sayles is best understood as a "critical realist," I'm disagreeing with Mark Bould, who in his study of Sayles holds that "he has been long engaged in developing American naturalist filmmaking" (6). Bould compares Sayles to Zola, in that the filmmaker's narrative method tends to present social problems "as social facts, as results, as *caput mortuum* of a social process," as Georg Lukács complained about the French naturalist ("Narrate or Describe?" 113–14). Sayles has been influenced by the American naturalist tradition, especially through the work of Nelson Algren, which he cites as an early influence on his fiction. But his films do not reveal a commitment to naturalism as an artistic form or as an ideology, lacking entirely any sense of the predetermined decline of individuals not possessed of the strongest traits. Sayles may often seem pessimistic, but this is better explained by Antonio Gramsci's maxim, "pessimism of intellect, optimism of the will," than it is by attributing to him a secret belief in biological determinism. Sayles's characters are never merely spectators, as Lukács believes Zola's are, but are always engaged in a struggle with the reality they confront. Still, political projects are meaningless without hope, since only a possibility of success, however limited or remote, makes such projects rational endeavors. Sayles's films never express complete hopelessness, but there are instances, which I discuss later, where their pessimism of the intellect comes close to negating any optimism of the will.

Lukács asserts, "The central aesthetic problem of realism is the adequate presentation of the complete human personality" (*Studies* 7). This is a view that Sayles might well share, because his films are peopled by an enormous range of characters and he strives to make them full-rounded. He takes his film characters so seriously that he writes biographies of them for his actors to read. And like the great Hungarian critic, Sayles understands that the human personality exists only within a definite social order. His films always give us characters who live in a particular time and place, belong to a recognizable class, and have a specific social role—almost always including work. But there are limits to how much a more or less orthodox Marxist like Lukács can enlighten us about the realism of a filmmaker who, whatever his personal relationship to the Marxist tradition, clearly does not regard it as the final truth about history and society. Lukács, the Hegelian Marxist, believed that it was possible to know society as a totality, and he believed that realists like Honoré de Balzac presented both human beings and society as "complete entities" (*Studies* 6). Sayles is skeptical of all claims to completeness, and would surely not claim it for any of his films. He may indeed accept the notion that society is a whole, but as a filmmaker all he can do is give us different perspectives or experiences of it. Unlike Lukács, Sayles brings no overarching preconception about the nature of reality to his films, assuming neither that history is a dialectical march toward utopia, nor that the current social arrangements are natural and inevitable.

Much of the formal experimentation featured in the independent films of the 1980s and 1990s is antirealist. It is hard to imagine that antirealist film theory, and the antirealism of poststructuralism more generally, did not have some influence on this trend. The 1970s critique of realism derived from poststructuralism, especially from Roland Barthes's dismissal of the referentiality of the text. For Barthes, what is of interest is not what a text can tell us about a world it claims to represent, but rather what it tells us about writing and reading—that is about itself and other texts. Thus in *S/Z*, Barthes asserts, "It is necessary to disengage the text from its exterior and its totality" (Quoted in MacCabe, "Realism" 140). If Barthes's position is extreme, it is not atypical of modernist and postmodernist criticism, which has consistently been skeptical of representation and which has read works of art primarily in terms of their relations to other works of art.

The critique that film theory made of Classical Hollywood cinema held that the process of making films seemed to be a transparent window on reality, the films offering the illusion of realism, i.e., an objective representation of reality, instead of the ideologically inflected representation it actually presented. Perhaps the most influential theorist of realism in film was Colin MacCabe. Like modernist critics of realism, he associated it with empiricism, but for him the chief problem was not realism's naïveté or lack of complexity, but its silent transmission of ideology. Hollywood films were seen as covertly ideological, and their realism was understood as an aspect of the false consciousness they were accused of purveying. This critique was applied to most fiction films, which were deemed realist despite the rather obvious unreality of many of them. The notion of Hollywood as a "dream factory" that triumphed by selling patent escapism largely disappeared from film studies at this time. "Realism" in 70s film theory was often called bourgeois, an assertion of a deep ideological connection between the form of Hollywood film and the ruling class that produced it.

Realism was not only accused of ignoring the fact of filmic mediation, but of claiming to present a complete picture of the world that was itself complete and without contradiction. Thus MacCabe argued that realism denies the viewer access to "contradictory positions available discursively to the subject" (64). The realist film offers a single point of view, for which it claims perfection, and which offers to the viewer an "imaginary plentitude" (67). Curiously then, this New Left criticism is attacking realism for doing exactly what Lukács claimed it ought to do, present the social totality. Lukács thought that realism presented the contradictions existing in society, while MacCabe wanted films that acknowledged the contradictions of discourse about society.

One of the effects of illusionistic realism was that style had to be subordinated to narrative so that the audience would focus only on the story and not think about the way it was presented to them. According to Robert Ray, "The ideological power of Classic Hollywood's procedure is obvious: under its sponsorship, even the most manufactured narratives came to seem spontaneous and 'real.' A spectator prevented from detecting style's role in a mythology's articulation could only accede to that mythology's 'truth'" (55). Film theorists therefore argued that anything that disrupted the illusion of realism, especially any violation of standard Hollywood visual conventions, could be construed as an act of resistance. Such violations would expose the supposed natural form of cinema as arbitrary and ideologically determined.

Sayles's work would seem to represent a solid rebuke to this attack on realism. His films are not only realist in intention, but by conscious design they subordinate style to narrative. Sayles's films suggest that the ideological work of Hollywood was not a function of its form, its failure to call attention to its own mediation, but to its narrow, affirmative vision, especially during the years of the production code. He sees the problem not as one of cinematic language, but of cinematic content. He might accept the idea that Hollywood films present a partial view of the world as if it were complete, but his answer to that is to show what is missing. His films depict a world quite different from "the cinema of affluence" of contemporary Hollywood (O'Sullivan in Carson, *Interviews* 87). Sayles's realism shows us a world that we are not expecting and in which we may not feel comfortable.

A significant element of Sayles's realism involves who and what he chooses to put on the screen. His films never focus on the rich or upper middle class in their own world, though they may include members of these groups, as in *Men with Guns* or *Casa de los babys*, when they are out of their element. His protagonists usually, however, are people we don't normally see on the screen, often those that are oppressed or marginalized: African Americans, Latinos both in the United States and in Latin America, lesbians, and, most consistently, working people. By the latter, I don't just mean the traditional industrial proletariat, though such workers do turn up in his films. Rather, Sayles shows work of all kinds, from housework to teaching, mining to restaurant and other service jobs, fishing to running a motel. Work is part of each of Sayles's films because, as he observed, quoting Studs Turkel, "You don't make love for eight hours a day, you don't eat either for hours a day—the only thing that you do for eight hours a day is sleep and work" (*Working*, quoted in Smith 76). Sayles's focus on work allows us to see the experience of capitalism that ordinary people have, and it demystifies the source of wealth by showing where goods and services actually come from. But work in Sayles's films is not always portrayed as alienated labor. Characters like the protagonists of *Limbo*, who love what they do, suggest the possibility of pleasure in work that capitalism denies to most workers.

Because of both the content of his films and the realist approach he takes to it, Sayles has often been taken to task for didacticism. But it should be remembered that, prior to the advent of modernism with its assumption of *l'art pour l'art*, it was assumed that great works of art would teach. As Philip Sidney put it of poetry, that they would "instruct and delight." The character of such instruction differed greatly from the Renaissance through the nineteenth century. The dominant view for much of the period held that works of art should present ideals rather than actualities, which is why realism in literature and painting was controversial. Sayles's discussions of his own work reveal that he thinks of himself as a teacher. He often chooses subjects, such as the West Virginia Coal War or the Philippine-American War, about which he believes people should know more. He speaks of certain characters in his films as playing the role of guide for the audience, for example Danny, the private investigator in *Silver City* (DVD interview, *The Making of Silver City*).

Sayles's sense of himself as teacher may be part of the reason for the extensive research he does for each new film. Accuracy of detail is something on which he prides himself, and, though historians have sometimes complained about things that he has left out of films such as *Matewan* and *Eight Men Out*, they have seldom accused him of getting the basic facts wrong. The same kind of devotion to accuracy goes into Sayles's explorations of places as disparate as County Donegal in Ireland and the Cajun country of Louisiana. While Hollywood is usually content to give us only a bit of the past or a place, often just its shiny surface, Sayles typically presents convincingly ordinary-looking objects and spaces, together with behavior and speech (including languages other than English) appropriate to the place and period. Moreover, his stories tell us something about the usually hidden economics and politics of the times and spaces he shows us.

Most viewers actually like learning new things from stories, as long as what they learn doesn't trouble their basic assumptions about the world. Because the facts that Sayles presents often are disruptive of common-sense assumptions, it is not surprising that he is sometimes described as a "political" filmmaker, unlike most others who are thought to leave politics out. But as Sayles observed in a 1987 interview,

> People forget that entertainment for entertainment's sake has a political message in it, too. It may not be an overt one but it's certainly there and it's an easy one to accept: "This is kind of a nice world, a nice way to think about ourselves." (O'Sullivan in Carson, *Interviews* 87).

Sayles clearly does have left-wing political assumptions, but he does not make propaganda films. Sayles's own perspective is often obvious, but urging that we accept that perspective is not the point of the film. Because that perspective is not typical of movies, however, people assume his films must be propaganda for it. But his films are much too open-ended and indeterminate to be easily read as urging a specific political position. As one of his interviewers observed, he "makes movies about problems nobody knows how to solve" (Scott in Carson, *Interviews* 129). He wants us to understand the problem, rather than to prescribe a way to fix it. This may be why Bould accuses him of naturalism and of treating social problems as ones that can never be solved. But the either/or of revolution or passive acceptance is not a premise Sayles would accept. His films often suggest that change is possible, but they don't imply it will be easy or that it can happen overnight. This attitude I call Sayles's political realism, by which I mean not that he holds a Machiavellian view of power, but that he sees the limitations that humans in power have despite any desire they have to do the right thing. Sayles presents a world in which injustice is the norm, where powerful nations, preeminently the United States, regard it as their right to control less powerful ones, yet he does not offer us a panacea in which these conditions would disappear. The lessons he teaches are historical, social, or human, and not usually ideological.

Indeed, it is not clear from his films or his statements to interviewers exactly what Sayles's own politics are. Marxists complain that he doesn't devote enough attention to the workings of capital, an accurate enough observation, though such attention would mean displacing the marginalized groups that normally people his films. To understand Sayles's politics, one should look at the period in which they were formed, the 1960s. While the New Left of that era reintroduced Marxism into American politics, it was as one theory among others. The story of the 1960s is the rise of new social movements, including civil rights and black power, feminism, and gay liberation. Sayles's perspective seems very much to have been formed out of these politics of representation and recognition, which he seems to regard as equal in importance to the more traditional goal of the left, redistribution. Despite his interest in work and workers, Sayles clearly does not believe that class is the root of all injustice. It is part of his realism to portray social relations as complex, involving different forms of power, privilege, and prestige, in addition to economic exploitation.

But if John Sayles does not hew to a single political program or theory, he nevertheless is best understood as a self-consciously political filmmaker. I take it that one of the reasons he has been so willing to discuss his films interviews, despite the fact that he is said not particularly to enjoy such conversations, is that he wants people to understand what he intended by them. Sayles apparently rejects entirely the various modernist dogmas that hold the text to be unparaphrasable and the author irrelevant to its meaning. As a result, I've assume here that what Sayles has to say about this own work is always relevant, and I have used these statements as a guide except in a few instances where I think the filmmaker has misjudged a likely audience response. Because I understand Sayles as self-consciously political, I have eschewed symptomatic readings, which by definition assume that the producer is unaware of his work's ideology. The practice of symptomatic reading is valid with regard to most films because they were not intended or understood as having an explicit politics, but it trivializes the explicit politics of films that have them. Of course, it is legitimate for critics to disagree with Sayles's politics, which Mark Bould, Rosa Linda Fregoso, and a few others clearly do. Yet these scholars don't present their criticism as political disagreement but precisely as a matter of Sayles's blindness to the "true" meanings of his films.

Sayles's realism is not itself best understood as a matter of form or genre. His identification with realism began with *Secaucus Seven* and it continues to this day. But if most of his films may be called realist, they are realist in different senses. Although he cites the Italian neorealists as an important influence, something born out by aspects of his filmmaking such as his use of nonprofessional or inexperienced actors for certain roles, he has not in the main imitated them. Rather, Sayles uses all manner of narrative conventions and film genres. He has made traditionally realist genres such as the comedy of manners, and he has invented new ones in which the social order of a city is depicted through multiple plotlines. What unites them are his goal of accuracy of representation and his commitment to showing things as they actually exist.

Paradoxically, Sayles sometimes tries to achieve these goals by making use of genres that have historically existed at some distance from realism, including science fiction, the Western, and the women's picture. On other occasions, he includes magical-realist elements in otherwise realist narratives. *The Secret of Roan Inish* contains fantastic elements that take it far beyond magical realism, and yet even this film involves a realism unusual in cinema of any kind, but especially in a film made for children. Perhaps most interestingly, in some of Sayles's films, such as *Lone Star* and *Limbo*, the mythic register of meaning is pushed to the foreground and the realist representation of the social seems to recede importance. It is my argument that all of Sayles's films are relatively realist when compared to most narrative cinema, and that his films in more mythic or melodramatic genres bend conventions to make them more realist. Even Sayles's deviations from a strictly realist mode of presentation can be understood as in the service of a larger realism, in that they enable a critical attitude. They allow perspectives on the world that would be prohibited by conventional realism, including the wishes and fears that are typically expressed in myths or dreams. Sayles wants us to understand the world we inhabit, but also to understand ourselves and our fellow humans as creatures capable of desire, will, and choice, though always under conditions not of our own making or choosing.

Beginnings: *Return of the Secaucus Seven*

John Sayles took a relatively unusual path to filmmaking, beginning as a writer of short stories and novels. Born and raised in Schenectady, New York, the child of two teachers, Sayles did not grow up a film buff. He read a great deal, and he played sports, hoping to pitch for the Pittsburgh Pirates when he grew up. He attended Williams College, a small, prestigious liberal arts institution in northwestern Massachusetts, where he read literary fiction and began to act in campus theatrical productions. At Williams he met several people who would be important to his film career, including Maggie Renzi and David Strathairn. He began to write fiction in college and had completed a novel by the time he graduated. After finishing his BA in 1972, he worked in many different jobs, most of them involving hard, physical labor, and he continued to send out stories to magazines. His work was noticed by an editor at the *Atlantic Monthly*, and by 1975 he had published his first novel, *Pride of the Bimbos.* A story he published in the *Atlantic* won an O. Henry Award that same year, and by 1977, his second novel, *Union Dues* was published.

Sayles had found an agent to help him publish *Union Dues*, and he used the agent's connections to find representation in Hollywood as a screenwriter, sending his screenplay for *Eight Men Out* as a sample. He got hired by Roger Corman, known as the "King of the B's" for the low-budget exploitation films his New World Pictures produced. Sayles ended up writing three films for Corman: *Piranha* (Joe Dante, 1978), *The Lady in Red* (Lewis Teague, 1979), and *Battle beyond the Stars* (Jimmy T. Murakmai, 1980). Lewis Teague subsequently hired him to write *Alligator* (1980) and Joe Dante to coscript *The Howling* (1981). Sayles established himself as a bankable screenwriter, and would develop into one of the best script doctors in Hollywood since Ben Hecht. But more important, the Corman screenplays and commissions from Teague and Dante gave him the money to direct his first film.

According to Peter Biskind, *Return of the Secaucus Seven* launched the independent film movement in American cinema (16). As Sayles himself put it, "At the time this movie was made, there really wasn't an independent film movement" (DVD commentary). The apparatus of distribution and promotion of such films remained largely to be developed. Robert Redford's Sundance Institute, for example, was founded in 1981, and it wouldn't hold a film festival until 1985. In the late 1970s, a few directors, such as John Cassavetes and Henry Jaglom, made films outside of the Hollywood system, but their films had limited outlets for exhibition. Although major cities had "art houses," that had featured foreign films since the 1960s and sometimes repertory houses that showed revivals, the recent consolidation of exhibition in the suburban multiplex meant that independent films tended to get screened only on college campuses and in other noncommercial venues. Under these circumstances, Sayles saw public television as the most promising outlet for such material.

Sayles's budget for the film was $40,000, the money coming from writing screenplays, and from the advance he received for *The Anarchists' Convention and Other Stories.* Although the finished film ended up costing $60,000, it grossed over $2 million, and this extraordinary return on investment made the industry sit up and take notice.

Secaucus Seven tells the story of a reunion of a group of friends who had opposed the Vietnam War and had a history of other activism. The film is set in a summerhouse Boston high-school teachers Mike (Bruce MacDonnald) and Katie (Maggie Renzi) have rented in the New Hampshire community where Mike had grown up. Their guests include J.T. (Adam LeFevre), a songwriter and would-be country singer; Frances (Maggie Cousineau), a medical student; Irene (Jean Passanante), an aide to a U.S. Senator; and her new boyfriend, Chip (Gordon Clapp), with whom she works. Maura (Karen Trott), has just split up with her live-in partner, Jeff (Mark Arnott), and both show up separately and unexpectedly. Chip is an outsider, the one character new to the group, and Sayles describes his role as a stand-in for the audience, which needs to be introduced to the others just as he does. The history of the groups' relationships with each other is explained to Chip by Mike:

> MIKE: Okay. Let me try to get it right the first time through. Katie and Maura went to college together. They were roommates with Lacey for a while. And I met Katie when I was going with Lacey, but we didn't get interested until much later. J.T. and Jeff went to Cornell together until Jeff dropped out to go into VISTA and J.T. just dropped out. Jeff and Maura met in VISTA, and they were living together when I was in VISTA working in Kentucky.

CHIP: Was Katie in VISTA?
MIKE: No, but she and Maura stayed good friends, and that's when I got to know her.
KATIE: Frances and Irene . . .
CHIP: Were in Rochester together.
MIKE: Right, and they lived downstairs from Katie and me in Boston for awhile, which is when she met J.T.
CHIP: I know about Irene and J.T.
MIKE: . . . who was visiting me, 'cos we met through Jeff in Kentucky. That was a long time ago, J.T. and Irene. Think you got it straight?
CHIP: Yeah, I think so. Only, who's Jeff?

Nothing much of consequence happens during the weekend. The group goes to see another old friend (Lacey) perform in a local summer theater. They play coed volleyball, and then the men play basketball while the women play Clue. They all go skinny-dipping, and later out to a local bar. On the way home, they find the carcass of a deer in the middle of the road and are arrested on suspicion of having poached it. The next day, everyone leaves.

While some of these activities, the sports primarily, provide visual interest, the most significant actions in the film involve the relationships of the characters. Maura and Jeff's breakup, which she announces on her arrival, precipitates most of the tensions that will occur among the group. As she puts it, "What's a reunion without a little drama." Frances, it is suggested is interested in J.T., but once Maura shows up, it becomes clear that he is interested in her. J.T and Maura have sex that night in the living room, where all three of them are sleeping. When Jeff shows up the next day there are tensions between him and J.T., because he does not consider his relationship with Maura to be over—though by the end of the film he will have accepted her decision.

Secaucus Seven approaches the condition of the case history in that it avoids the familiar modes of emplotment, tragedy, comedy, satire, and romance. Although the film has been accurately classified as a "comedy of modern manners," "comedy" here describes the film's mood and its scenes rather than its plot. According to Northrop Frye, the comic plot ends in marriage as a celebration of the renewal of the community, but *Secaucus Seven* ends with the dissolution of a relationship, while none of the new intimacies seem likely to continue. However, a connection to the comic may remain in the continued friendship of this group despite their history of coupling and recoupling that must now stand for community. The fact that the group can reconstitute itself only once a year implies that community is difficult in contemporary America.

Though the characters are associated with the 1960s student Left, clearly the most significant event of the decade for them was the "sexual revolution." The film's main concern is how to deal with the new landscape of interpersonal relationships created by the pill, the women's liberation movement, and the decline of the stigmas against premarital sex and cohabitation. This suggests that the movie is realist in the sense that John Updike has characterized much contemporary American fiction, which focuses on "domestic morality and sexual politics that interested [William Dean] Howells" (Updike 189). Indeed, as Richard Corliss observed in his 1980 *Time* review, the film covers some of the same geography and themes, "They're turning 30, jogging toward the compromises of early middle age—Updikescent—and out of the corner of their minds they wonder how much fun that will be."

It is worth emphasizing that in 1979, when *Secaucus Seven* was made, living together out of wedlock was still a new social reality. The film's focus on these issues is highlighted by several exchanges early on. The opening scenes involve dialogue between Mike and Katie while they are readying the house for their guests. A major concern is where people will sleep. Irene and Chip will get the second bedroom in recognition of their new relationship, but should the mattress be placed on the floor to avoid embarrassing noises and the chance of the bed collapsing? After Frances arrives, Katie mentions to her that she noticed that she had packed a diaphragm. Not only does this indicate Frances's expectation of sex, but that she has gone off the pill. Frances explains that one of her exam questions was about adverse reactions to the drug, which she proceeds to list. Later, when the group encounters Mike's old friend Howie (John Sayles) and his wife, Carol (Marisa Smith) who have three small children, Katie remarks, "There but for the grace of Oval 21."

Besides emphasizing the relative novelty of oral contraceptives, this remark points to significant social changes that the pill helped to bring about. It allowed the women in this group to postpone childbearing and also marriage. While the group includes several long-term couples, none has obtained legal sanction for their relationship. One of the film's concerns is to explore Mike and Katie's domestic life and to show us something of how their relationship works. The division of labor in the opening scene shows both continuity and change. While Mike is shown fixing a toilet and Katie making a bed, Mike also takes responsibility for cleaning. Later, he will be shown cooking. These represent real if perhaps small changes in the household division of labor in a couple that could easily be married, but has chosen not to be. The influence of second-wave feminism on the characters and Sayles is clear from these details. The skinny-dipping scene seems to reflect an awareness of feminist film theory, as only the men are shown naked, and the women are depicted as commenting on the men's bodies (see figure 2).

The marriage-like character of Mike and Katie's relationship contrasts with the situations of the other members of the group. Although Jeff and Maura had been living together for a long time, the film focuses on their new condition. The relative ease of the transition is implicitly contrasted with the divorce that would have been necessary had they been married. Maura's decision to have sex with J.T. emphasizes the degree to which she is emotionally unencumbered, while we later see her and Jeff calmly making plans to divide up the small amount of property they share. Besides Maura and J.T., Frances will hook up with Ron (David Strathairn), another of Mike's local friends. The ease of these one-night stands also reflects the then new morality. There is nothing that requires that these relationships continue to justify them. However, that these women have had many partners troubles Chip, as we learn from a scene where Irene confesses to having been with Ron. That women can be as sexually experienced as men is another new reality of the 1970s.

The comparison that Katie makes between herself and Carol has a strong class dimension, as the film makes more explicit later. Sayles said, "Class in America is a shifty thing, but it does exist," and *Secaucus Seven* makes a point of exploring class differences (DVD commentary). The pattern that Howie and Carol followed of getting married and having children early in their lives was typical of the 1950s for Americans of most classes, but by this time it has become the norm only of the working class. These differences are explored in conversation among Ron, Howie, and Mike at the bar. Howie explains both the limits on his life his family entails but also the pride he feels in his children. As he sums it up, "It's not that it's bad. It's all the work, all the time that you got to

Figure 2. Maura (Karen Trott) and Katie (Maggie Renzi) watch the men skinny-dipping in *Return of the Secaucus Seven.*

put in." Since Howie works a second job as a late-night hotel clerk on weekends, we understand that his time is restricted by more than just the need to be with his family. Moreover, Howie doesn't seem to have any ambitions to move beyond his current situation. We can't imagine how his life might change. This distinguishes him from most of the members of the reunion, who still see their lives as in development. That's true even of Ron, whose working-class status as an auto mechanic is belied to some extent by his manner of speaking and his sense of irony about his own career—something Howie lacks entirely.

The class differences explored here are not the ones typical of Hollywood, where love is often portrayed as capable of bridging the gap between the very rich and the poor. The high gloss that passes for middle class in most movies is missing. The cast, which consisted mainly of actors Sayles knew from his acting in summer stock, lacks any then-recognizable faces, and this ordinariness is consistent with the film's ordinary settings and spare plot. Mainly shot in an empty ski lodge in North Conway, New Hampshire, *Secaucus Seven* gives us resolutely unglamorous images—but they are not images of poverty or deprivation either. The milieu of the film is genuinely middle-class, its characters mainly being employed as teachers and in other professional roles requiring education but paying modest salaries.

Sayles observes that the men in the film are "downwardly mobile," while the women are upwardly mobile, if only because they have careers where their mothers did not (Smith 56). Both have chosen these paths, the men having rejected the temptations of high-paying professional or business careers for the rewards of doing work that they believe contributes to the social good. This ethos is especially striking as the film was released on the cusp of the Reagan Era when such choices would be regarded as distinctly unfashionable. Before the end of the 1980s, Michael Douglas's Gordon Gekko from *Wall Street* (Oliver Stone, 1987), whose motto is "greed is good," will have become the poster boy for the decade.

Unlike most men in American movies, those in this group are not mainly preoccupied with their own jobs or careers. Sayles said that he made the film in part as a response to obituaries from the 1960s (Smith 57), and that it is about people "trying to keep their idealism together" (Smith 56). The central problem nobody knows how to solve in *Secaucus Seven* is how to maintain one's idealism in the face of the need to earn a living. The film then is not about the big political issues associated with the 1960s such as Vietnam or civil rights. We know where the group stood on those issues. Sayles describes them as the "foot soldiers of the anti-war movement." Their radicalism is for the most part suggested rather than asserted. Mike, for example, talks of beginning his high-school history course with the Boston police strike of 1919, and in conducting a mock class with the group, he uses phrases such as "running dog imperialist," which we are meant to recognize as clichés of a bygone moment.

There are some political discussions among the characters, but they seem mainly designed to suggest a range of political positions rather than to endorse any one of them. Chip and Jeff, for example, have an argument about whether working within the system can result in real change or is just a form of cooptation. Although Chip is clearly "politically straight," as someone calls him in the film, Sayles does not take sides in this exchange, and it is significant that it takes place with Jeff, of whom Sayles says there is a dark edge. Jeff works as counselor in a drug rehabilitation center, but he is carrying some heroin one of his clients gave him. He apparently can't decide whether to use it or not, but the possibility is suggested that he could become an addict himself.

Jeff and Maura's history of radicalism is displayed when they are asked to tell the arresting officer after the poaching bust of any prior arrests. It turns out they have had many, though apparently no convictions. It is in this scene in the police station where the film's title is explained. The group had been driving in a borrowed station wagon from Boston to a big antiwar demonstration in Washington when they were stopped in Secaucus, New Jersey, for the crime of looking like they were going to the demonstration. The cop finds an ounce of marijuana in the back of the car (left there by the car's owner), and the whole group has to spend the night in jail. Since the men and women are in adjoining cells, they spend the night making jokes about being the Secaucus Seven (an allusion to antiwar leaders tried as the Chicago Seven) and reciting lines from old movies, including *The Salt of the Earth* (Herbert J. Biberman, 1954) a film about an actual strike at the Empire Zinc Mine in New Mexico made by members of the blacklisted Hollywood Ten. The episode is presented as a bonding experience, and the abortive character of their trip to the demonstration is perhaps a metaphor for the failure of the movement to bring about the radical change they desired. These characters are aware that the revolution is not coming soon, and they are trying to figure out how to imagine other paths to the goals in which they continue to believe.

The Return of the Secaucus Seven may be best known today as the film that inspired Lawrence Kasdan's *The Big Chill* (1983), and that much more widely seen film may have caused Sayles's work to be misremembered. Unlike *The Big Chill*, *Return of the Secaucus Seven* is not a nostalgia film; while its characters spend a bit of time recalling their younger days, they are mainly concerned with the present and future. And, although Kasdan's movie is notable for its extensive use of hit records from the 1960s, Sayles uses only original music having no temporal associations. *The Big Chill* is about the memory of the 1960s; *Secaucus Seven* is about the lasting impact of social change associated with that decade. In Sayles's view, the two films differ in that Kasdan's movie is about characters who have lost their idealism, or never had any to begin with (Smith 56). *The Big Chill* features characters who are upwardly mobile and who are middle class only in Hollywood's much inflated sense. The host of its reunion owns a chain of athletic shoe stores and lives in a mansion; other characters include a Tom Selleck–like TV star and a journalist for *People*. *The Big Chill*'s star-studded cast and glossy production values fit with this elite stratum of society, making it the antithesis of Sayles's low-budget ensemble piece.

Sayles's limited budget should be seen as the condition for his film's distinctive realism, and for many of its most interesting stylistic features. The low budget meant not only that Sayles would need to hire young, inexperienced actors, but that the film would have to be shot quickly and in 16 mm. Sayles says one of his influences in making the film was Robert Altman's *Nashville* (1975), which had "a million subplots motivated by cuts" (Smith 51). Sayles knew that he would not have the money to shoot much action or be able to move the camera very much. He therefore decided to use editing to inject visual excitement into the story. Most sequences of the film crosscut showing more or less simultaneous action and avoiding the sense that one is watching a filmed play. The cuts are often connected by bits of dialogue, as near the end of the film when Mike and Katie are discussing whether Frances will return that evening since she left the bar with Ron. Katie indicates she can't see Frances's interest, and Mike responds, "What's wrong with Ron," on which Sayles cuts to Chip saying "Ron?" to Irene. This linking of scenes through dialogue creates a sense not only of cinematic continuity, but also the sense of connections among the group.

Secaucus Seven also bears some resemblance to Italian neorealism, and to the more recent films of directors such as Mike Leigh or Ken

Loach. These films are defined by a radical rejection, not only of Hollywood's glossy style and look, but also of its usual genres. Sayles said he would have been happy had the film looked more like an MTV reality show, but that the style of "nervous" camera and of out-of-focus shots was years away (DVD commentary). The neorealists used nonprofessionals to cast their films. Sayles cast a few parts with people who had done no professional acting, but most roles were filled by people who had worked in summer-stock theater and the like. The effect, however, is quite similar, in that we are not watching stars or even actors whom we are likely to have seen before and thus associate with the movies. According to Sayles, "Shooting it, I had to say that the first priority was that the people come across as very real, that you don't feel that you're watching actors. In fact, I had unknowns, with the advantage that people would think they must all be playing themselves, even though none of them are. I could go a little further in the direction of documentary than you can with known actors" (Chute in Carson, *Interviews* 6).

It must also be observed, however, that the lighter tone of *Secaucus Seven* differs from that of the generally more serious neorealists. Sayles thought of the film both as something that Hollywood studios would not make and as an "audition piece," a film that would demonstrate "production, writing, and directing values that they would recognize as good for their purposes" (Chute in Carson, *Interviews* 5). This combination reflects a sensibility that sets Sayles apart from independent filmmakers in the Jarmusch mode, whose goal is to be formally distinct from Hollywood. Sayles has been more ambivalent about Hollywood. While he has made films that Hollywood won't, he had also made use of its forms, techniques, and resources.

Sayles had not expected *Secaucus Seven* to have theatrical distribution, and, in fact, he was a bit unsure what to do with the film once he had made it. His first break came through Maggie Renzi's mother, whose friend, Adrienne Mancia worked at the Museum of Modern Art. They screened the film for her, and she recommended it to a colleague with whom she programmed the Museum's New Directors/New Films festival. After accepting the film, it was suggested to Sayles that he also submit to Filmex, a Los Angeles Festival. The film did well at both festivals, receiving a positive review from Vincent Canby of the *New York Times*. Moreover, the festivals resulted in contacts with small distributors who were interested in taking on the film. One of them, Randy Finley offered to put up $20,000 to blow it up to 35 mm, and to distribute it on the West Coast. The film opened in September of 1980, and, though its initial New York run was disappointing, it did well in Seattle, where Finley was based, and other cities. It made the "10-best lists" for 1980 of the *Boston Globe*, the *Los Angeles Times*, and *Time*, and it was nominated for Best Comedy Written Directly for Screen by the Writer's Guild. For a return engagement in New York in March 1981, the *New York Times* ran a highly complimentary feature on Sayles by Aljean Hartmetz, and the film had an extended run this time around.

Establishing a Career: *Lianna* and *Baby It's You*

The early 1980s saw Sayles experimenting with different strategies of film production. He could not keep making movies year in and year out on budgets of $60,000, so he tried both independent financing and working under a studio contract. By 1985, he and producer Maggie Renzi had established a record for making financially successful and critically acclaimed low budget films. The success of *Secaucus Seven* earned Sayles two studio contracts for films that never got made, but neither the major studios nor any other companies were interested in making *Lianna*, the story he wanted to make next. This is another indication of the undeveloped state of independent filmmaking and distribution in the early 1980s. As Sayles put it in 1998, "Today, if you had a thing that was a hit at Sundance the way *Secaucus Seven* was a hit, you'd have a six-picture deal or something like that" (Smith 68). As a result, Sayles and his producers, Jeffrey Nelson and Maggie Renzi, had to raise all of the money for *Lianna* beyond the $50,000 the director himself invested. They had hoped to have $800,000, which would have allowed the film to be shot in 35 mm, but after a year and a half, they decided to go with 16 mm on a budget of $300,000.

Lianna is about a woman's discovery of her lesbian sexuality and her coming out, a story that Sayles says grew out of his observation of the difficulties couples had divorcing with kids. The screenplay was written before the one for *Secaucus Seven* in a burst of creativity in 1977 and 1978 during which Sayles also wrote *Matewan* and *Eight Men Out*. Sayles says the script "was not originally necessarily about gay women or that world, and that wasn't what brought me to it. It was the women's movement and seeing an awful lot of marriages and relationships break up" (Smith 68). He chose to make *Lianna* lesbian because it provided a situation in which a woman would face the threat of losing custody of her children. The film continues several concerns of *Secaucus Seven*, including what it means to turn 30 and to deal with the new realities of sex and marriage.

Even more than *Secaucus Seven*, *Lianna* deserves to be classified with other "relationship stories" of the 1970s, such as Woody Allen's *Annie Hall* (1977) and *Manhattan* (1979), and Paul Mazursky's *An Unmarried Woman* (1978).[1] Like these films, it could be called a study of manners, but unlike them, it does not rely heavily on humor to make the failure of the relationships it depicts less emotionally wrenching. Sayles has described the film as "a traditional romantic story," in which a woman ends a relationship, falls in love with someone else, and experiences another breakup. What he says is different is not that she ends up falling in love with another woman, but that a lot of the things that in Hollywood get done in a montage with soft focus are here dramatized (DVD commentary). Allen and Mazursky dramatize some of these moments—or they have their characters explain them—but they also make use of romantic images augmented not only by an upper–middle-class milieu, but also by the familiar and often extraordinarily attractive stars they cast and the cities chosen as settings.

In fact, while *Lianna* does deal with the same subjects as films we would normally call romantic, it does not tell its story romantically. At the core of romance as a plot form are the obstacles to a couple's love, which are in comedy overcome or in tragedy not overcome. Those obstacles serve to intensify the passion of the story and to make the outcome a genuine climax. Although there are many obstacles to Lianna's (Linda Griffiths) love for Ruth (Jane Halleran), they do not provide the backbone of the narrative. That consists of the series of problems that Lianna is forced to confront, first as a wife and mother, and later as a lesbian and single woman. She finds solutions to each of these problems, but the solutions are not panaceas, because every solution comes with new problems. Even Lianna's realization of her sexuality, which is portrayed as unambiguously positive, is not represented as the end of her problems. Sayles has said some of what he was trying to get at was that figuring out who you are sexually doesn't necessarily solve all your problems. "Your relationships aren't necessarily what you dreamed them to be" (DVD commentary). As explained elsewhere, "One of Lianna's problems was that she was a student and married to her teacher. Who does she fall in love with? Another teacher" (Smith 70). Yet this repetition is not treated as an incurable neurosis or as a tragic mistake. It is rather something from which Lianna can learn, a mistake she is less likely to make again. *Lianna* then is an antiromantic—or realist—look at marriage and lesbian courtship.

Although *Lianna* clearly has higher production values than *Secaucus Seven*, it retains a similar visual realism. The images may be even grainier, and while the locations include several middle-class homes and apartments occupied by professors, being shot in Hoboken, New Jersey rather than North Conway, New Hampshire, gives it overall a grittier look. The college where most of the characters either work or study is spare and functional and lacks any sense of the groves of academe. The scenes in My Way Tavern, the film's women's bar, were shot in a Hoboken sports bar, and it is a distinctly working-class setting (see figure 3). The apartment Lianna rents after she moves out was a vacant flat the look of which Sayles says they could not have come up with had they designed a set for the scenes there. It looks to be a sort of railroad flat, and, before Lianna decorates it, it can only be described as dreary. "There really is an energy, and a tone, and a vibe, that you get from real places that's hard to recreate on a sound stage" (DVD commentary).

Part of the point of the downscale look of these settings is that the breakup of Lianna's marriage means that she will have to live on a much smaller income. "A split up . . . is not just an emotional thing. It's also an economic thing" (DVD commentary). This very real aspect of divorce has been ignored by most other relationship stories. Compare Erica's (Jill Clayburgh) situation in *An Unmarried Woman*, where she seems to lose neither standard of living nor status. She finds an apartment so big and bright that the rent it would command in New York would be well beyond the means of a newly divorced, middle-class woman. While Erica finds work in an art gallery, where she picks up an artist played by Alan Bates, Lianna after a search finds work as a checkout clerk in the

Figure 3. Ruth (Jane Hallaren) and Lianna (Linda Griffiths) at the My Way Tavern.

local grocery. Her pink work uniform demarcates this at least temporary fall in status. As always in Sayles, class is a visible reality here.

Lianna's postdivorce problems are not depicted as purely economic. She is thirty, and, according to Sayles, she has to grow up quickly after she leaves her husband. She needs to learn how to find a job and live on her own (DVD commentary). *Secaucus Seven* had also dealt with people turning thirty who hadn't entirely grown up, in their case because they had delayed childbearing. Lianna has children, but because of the unequal role she played in her marriage and of her having left college after one year to marry Dick (Jon DeVries), she relied on him to take care of her financially. She has remained Dick's pupil, his research assistant, and his typist. The class she is taking with Ruth on child psychology represents an awakening of her own intellectual interests, as well as becoming the occasion for her sexual awakening. One implication of this is that marriage must have kept many women infantilized until the women's movement and the liberalized divorce laws of the 1960s. Much of what goes on in *Lianna* is an implicit critique of gender inequality. The men in the film range from the unredeemable Dick, to his film-professor colleague, the semidecent Jerry Carlson (Sayles), to the football coach and husband of Lianna's best friend—the most sympathetic but still very much the stereotypical coach. In other words, men like many of those in *Secaucus Seven*, who had also been educated by the women's movement, are missing here as they probably were in much of late-1970s America.

Sayles's difficulties in interesting the studios in *Lianna*, of course, also stemmed from its subject matter. The studios did not believe that a film about lesbianism would have commercial appeal at a time when there had been few open and sympathetic depictions of lesbians in Hollywood movies. In 1982, *Personal Best* (Robert Towne) was released by Warner Brothers with a mixed critical reception and weak box office. While it treated a lesbian relationship sympathetically, the protagonist, played by Mariel Hemingway, decides in the end that she is heterosexual. Despite the fact that there had always been some disguised or implicit lesbians in Hollywood films, the making of *Lianna* must be regarded as a radical statement. It may be hard to recall just how edgy this material would have been in the late 1970s or early 1980s, when many states still had sodomy laws and very few localities offered civil rights protections to gays and lesbians. *Lianna* doesn't advocate anything with regard to these issues, but by portraying a lesbian protagonist sympathetically and realistically, the film may have done more to help the cause than if it had.

Lianna received strong reviews from mainstream critics, but its reception by lesbian and feminist critics, was in general much less welcoming.[2] This is perhaps unsurprising in a period when identity politics often insisted that who said something was more important than what was said, and Sayles was both male and straight. Moreover, the lack of lesbians in film—on screen and behind the camera—meant that such critics would inevitably want any film in which they appeared to make up for as much of this absence as possible. That is an impossible demand to be placed on any one film, especially one as modest as *Lianna*, which, as Sayles admitted, is a limited take on lesbian life. Since he didn't have intimate acquaintance with lesbian subculture, he made a film about someone who was also unfamiliar with it.

Despite the favorable reviews, *Lianna* did not do as well as *Secaucus Seven* at the box office. Sayles attributes this to his difficulty in finding a distributor and to the unfortunate timing of his finally finding one.

United Artists Classics picked up the film, but soon after it opened, its executives left to form Orion Classics. UA Classics became a kind of corporate orphan, and the film was not well supported. In some cities, *Lianna* opened after Sayles's next film, *Baby, It's You*. Nevertheless, the film still grossed $1.5 million, or nearly five times what it cost to make.

Also released in 1983, *Baby, It's You* is to date the only film Sayles has made under a studio contract, and hence, the only film over which he did not have complete artistic control. The final cut was his, but only after the studio had someone else unsuccessfully reedit the film in an attempt to respond to comments of preview audiences. The film is also an outlier in Sayles's corpus because it is based on a story written by someone else, Amy Robinson, an actress who brought the project to Sayles, and who also produced it with Griffin Dunne. Sayles indicates that the difficulties he had with the project were as much a result of differences between him and Robinson as between him and Paramount. "Amy always said, 'The problem with this movie is that I think that it's a romance, you think it's a class-conflict movie, and Paramount thinks it's a teenage sex comedy—so something's got to give somewhere'" (Smith 80). While Paramount clearly did not get its sex comedy, the division between romance and class-conflict film was never fully resolved. The film contains only partly reconciled elements of each. For this and other reasons, it is Sayles's least successfully realized project.

Working with a budget of $2.9 million gave Sayles the chance to shoot in 35 mm, to hire more experienced talent both in front of and behind the camera, and to be able to make use of a wider range of locations, including Miami Beach. The result, however, is not a film that exudes studio polish. None of the actors were stars, and the locations were most often in New Jersey cities, including Hoboken and Newark. While these factors contribute a degree of realism of the sort found in Sayles's previous films, the story is much less a slice of life than they were. Like them, *Baby, It's You* is a film about relationships, and about new gender relations represented from a woman's perspective. But unlike most of Sayles's films, the relationship here is implausible, seeming like something out of an old Hollywood comedy.

Baby, It's You is the story of Jill Rosen (Rosanna Arquette), the daughter of a physician and a homemaker who once aspired to be an actress, and the Sheik (Vincent Spano), a working-class kid who wants to grow up to be Frank Sinatra. They meet each other in high school, where Jill is something of a model student, and the Sheik finds himself after having been expelled from several other institutions. Set in the mid 1960s in Trenton, New Jersey, the film contrasts the comfortable upper–middle-class life of the Rosens, with the working-class milieu that the Sheik inhabits. His father is a garbage collector, and his mother keeps the Sheik's expensive-looking suits pressed. The Sheik walks around the school like he owns the place, flouting the rules that require students to go to class. He sees Jill for the first time and immediately asks her out. Jill refuses at first, but she is clearly intrigued by him and won over by his persistence. They fall for each other, but the relationship is difficult. After Jill graduates, she attends Sarah Lawrence College, while the Sheik has to hightail it to Florida to avoid being arrested for burglary. He takes a job washing dishes, while occasionally getting the chance to entertain the restaurant's customers by lip-synching Frank Sinatra records. Jill finds college difficult emotionally, and she goes to visit her old boyfriend. It becomes clear to her there that the relationship can go no further, but the Sheik doesn't see it. After an actual singer makes his lip-synching redundant, he steals a car to go see Jill. After he trashes her dorm room, she tells him it's over, but he takes her to the big school dance when her date stands her up. The film ends with the couple dancing to "Strangers in the Night" played by a rock band (see figure 4).

The film is Sayles's first film to be set in the past, and it is one of a number of films in the 1970s and 1980s that attempt to re-create relatively recent periods in American history, among them *American Graffiti* (George Lucas, 1973), and *Dirty Dancing* (Emile Ardolino, 1987), which also are about the 1960s. Fredric Jameson has called *American Graffiti* "the inaugural film of [a] new aesthetic discourse," the "nostalgia film," or what French critics have called *le mode rétro*, taken by him to be a prime example of the postmodern effacement of history (xvii, 18–19). Jameson argues that "nostalgia films restructure the whole issue of pastiche and project it onto a collective and social level, where the desperate attempt to appropriate a missing past is now refracted through the iron law of fashion change and the emergent ideology of the generation." Jameson's emphasis is on the way such films render the "'past' through

Figure 4. Jill (Rosanna Arquette) and the Sheik (Vincent Spano) dance to "Strangers in the Night."

stylistic connotation, conveying 'pastness' by the glossy qualities of the image, and 1930s-ness or 1950s-ness by the attributes of fashion" (19).

Despite its period setting, *Baby, It's You* is clearly not a nostalgia film in Jameson's sense, or any other for that matter. It is their glossiness or prettiness that marks Jameson's examples as interested in surface rather than historical depth, but *Baby, It's You* is gritty in its very photography. Even the beach scenes—shot in both New Jersey and Florida—do not make one wish one was there. While visually the film avoids anachronism, it is not focused on the details of period fashions or other consumer goods.

The period that writer/director John Sayles depicts is one for which we are encouraged to feel only the most ambivalent longing. Rather than depicting "the time of one's life" (as one of *Dirty Dancing*'s songs has it), *Baby, It's You* tells a story fraught with false hopes, failed dreams, emotional turmoil, and confused identities. Neither Jill's difficulty in adjusting to college life, nor the Sheik's self-confessed lack of a future register as experiences they or we would want to relive. Yet, in spite of its depiction of mundane social space and its frank acknowledgment of class oppression—the film offers little hope regarding its working-class hero's future—*Baby, It's You* seems not only less hopeful, but less critical and less political than *Dirty Dancing*.

Another way in which *Baby, It's You* avoids the nostalgia trap is by not using period music to re-create the past aurally, as did, in different ways and degrees *American Graffiti*, *The Big Chill*, and *Dirty Dancing*. In Sayles's film, music is less significant than it is in those, though at first it may seem to play much the same role. The songs that we first hear are ones from the early to mid-1960s and thus ones to which Jill could plausibly be listening. The title, *Baby, It's You*, is taken from the song the Shirelles recorded in 1961, and the film uses a good bit of girl-group music that perhaps was chosen to emphasize that this is mainly a young woman's story. Music is portrayed as important in the lives of both characters. We see Jill lip-synching "Stop in the Name of Love," by the Supremes in her bedroom in front of a mirror. The Sheik is obsessed with Frank Sinatra, and his music is used diegetically in a number of scenes.

But in *Baby, It's You* popular records often function like classic film scores, serving to augment the emotional character of the scenes. Thus the film uses anachronistic Bruce Springsteen recordings from the 1970s to give us a sense of the Sheik's world and his feelings. Moreover, the other films portray a unified musical field, while Sayles uses music to reveal two cultural conflicts. One becomes apparent in the Sheik's obsession with Sinatra, which renders impossible the sense of generational solidarity cultivated by the other films. This point is driven home by having the rock band play "Strangers in the Night" in the film's concluding scene. The second conflict is expressed by the changes in the music as the decade gets older and the heroine moves from her New Jersey high school to Sarah Lawrence College. While the earlier music would fit perfectly into the other three films, the later music includes songs such as Al Kooper's "(First I Heard Her Say) Wake Me Shake Me" and the Velvet Underground's "Venus in Furs." These musical ruptures interfere with any nostalgia effect that *Baby, It's You* might otherwise produce.

Sayles uses Frank Sinatra versus rock in its various forms to represent class divide between Jill and the Sheik. Yet this choice seems contrived. Although the Sheik's tastes in music and his identification with Sinatra are hardly impossible, they surely are not typical. Springsteen's songs from the 1970s are about a similar milieu to the Sheik's, but it is impossible to imagine any of his characters listening to Sinatra. But if the Sheik's musical tastes are unlikely, so is Jill's relationship with him. We can understand why she might have been attracted to him physically and to the forbidden fruit he represents, but the movie wants us to believe that their relationship is much deeper for both of them. This is plausible for the Sheik given his narrow expectations of women, but it is not for her. If he had been working-class but hip—rather than square—we might have been persuaded. As it is, all one can think about through the last half of the movie is, "what can this smart, beautiful, and ambitious woman see in this guy?"

Still, Sayles deserves credit for portraying the class divide as too wide for the two lovers to bridge. Cross-class romance has been a staple of Hollywood comedies from *It Happened One Night* (Frank Capra, 1934) to *Pretty Woman* (Garry Marshall, 1990), but in real life, cross-class marriage has always been uncommon. The depiction of the unbridgeable class divide, however, also represents a limitation on the film's politics in that it fails to convey any sense of hope. *Baby, It's You* is best understood as a kind of bildungsroman, a portrait of an artist as a young girl. And Sayles's difficulty with the material may in part have been due to the fact that he does not conceive of himself as an artist. Sayles has said that *Baby, It's You* is one of the two films he has made that were closest to his own experience growing up (Smith 79), but neither of the protagonists has much in common with him. Perhaps the fact that Sayles was not working from his own story was as big a problem as having to conform to the studio's demands.

The reviews for *Baby, It's You* ranged from mixed to positive, with the more prominent critics Roger Ebert and Vincent Canby the most positive. The *New York Times* actually gave the film two positive notices, the first by Janet Maslin, who noted, "well-chosen details of a 1960's adolescence are captured by John Sayles with characteristically witty precision." David Ansen in *Newsweek* praised the film for "trenchant social details that Sayles, who is attuned to every nuance of class, is so good at" (78). But *Baby, It's You*, despite the good reviews and the weight of a major studio behind it, in Sayles's words "tanked," grossing only $1.3 million in the United States (Smith 105).

The Brother from Another Planet and Springsteen Videos

Sayles had hoped to next make *Matewan*, the screenplay that he had written in the late 1970s, but he was unable to raise the $4 million he needed. In 1983, he had been awarded a MacArthur Fellowship, giving him tax-free income of $35,000 a year for five years. Having that cushion to live on allowed Sayles to again use money earned as a screenwriter for hire to make *The Brother from Another Planet.* So, like *Secaucus Seven* and *Lianna*, this film had to be made on a tiny budget, in this case, $250,000. Yet, as a serious sci-fi comedy about an extraterrestrial escaped slave, the film represented a significant departure from his previous three films. Here the previous focus on gender and generation is replaced by race, and the antigeneric realism of his earlier films gives way to a genre-bending fantasy, albeit while retaining many elements of realism.

In tackling racism and the oppression of African Americans, Sayles is addressing issues that had been almost as absent from the screen as had lesbianism. In 1984, Spike Lee's first commercial film, *She's Gotta Have It*, was still two years away. And, while racism had been addressed seriously on occasion since *To Kill a Mocking Bird* (Robert Mulligan, 1962), films set mainly within an African American neighborhood had been rare, the "blacksploitation" cycle of the 1970s notwithstanding. The film features a mostly black cast and a largely black crew, and it was shot by Ernest Dickerson, who had been the cinematographer on Lee's student film, *Joe's Bed-Sty Barbershop: We Cut Heads. Brother* was mainly shot in Harlem, and one of its strongest elements is its sense of place. Although Sayles had previously shot on location, in this instance the location itself is significant.

Brother opens with a scene in the alien's spacecraft, the design of which is worthy of Ed Wood. We see a bunch of neon-looking lights and some indecipherable letters in a lighted display accompanied by hokey electronic noises. It is a distinctly low-tech rendering of a high-tech environment, and this coming after *Star Wars* had raised everyone's expectations for such gadgetry. Because this will be a comedy, however, the obviously artificial scene is not out of keeping with the tone of the rest of the film.

When the ship splashes down, we see a sign saying "Ellis Island Immigration Center." The next shot shows the Statue of Liberty in the background as we see the Brother (Joe Morton) climb out of the water. This alien is arriving at the most famous port of entry for immigrants to the United States, and both the statue and sign remind viewers of the idea that we are a nation of immigrants who came here seeking liberty. The Brother, however, will find no welcome at the Immigration Center, which in 1984 was an empty ruin. But Sayles also reminds us that Ellis Island was never a happy place. The Brother touches the walls of the Center, and he is able to feel and hear the pain of those who passed through it—or were sent back to the old country. This opening makes it clear that *Brother* is not just about race, but also about the experience of alienation characteristic of the migrant and other oppressed internal minorities.[3]

In addition to his ability to experience the past by touching objects remaining from it—a special power that radically distinguishes him from most Americans—who seem entirely disconnected from history—we learn that the Brother has the ability to regenerate his limbs. After spending the night on the island, he manages to hitch a ride on a passing ferry and finds himself in Manhattan. Eventually, he walks into Harlem, where we see him try to figure out the rules of this strange world. Spying a display of fruit at a corner market, he picks up an apple and bites into it, causing the owner to chase him away. He comes back and observes a customer paying for the fruit with bills that the owner puts into her cash register. While she is away from the register, the Brother uses another of his alien powers to open it merely by laying his hands upon it. He takes some bills out, and then offers them to the owner gesturing that he wants some fruit. This episode reveals that money is not something with which he is familiar, and so Sayles reminds us that there is nothing natural about it.

Though the Brother drops the money when the owner chases him, a cop on his beat is alerted and pursues him down the street. The Brother here learns another fact of life for the black residents of Harlem, that the police regard them mainly as their opponents. The Brother escapes by leaping up to a second-story flagpole, demonstrating another of his unusual talents. The cops' pursuit anticipates that of the interplanetary bounty hunters, the men in black (John Sayles and David Strathairn), who will be chasing the Brother throughout most of the film. The

Brother finds a place of rest in Odell's bar, where he meets a group of regulars who try to figure out his story but ultimately accept him despite their failure to do so. It is here we learn that the Brother is mute, but that he can hear and understand human language. Morton was widely praised for his ability to communicate his reactions without speaking them, and the film often reminds us of the pleasures of silent cinema.

There is a bar scene in each of Sayles's first four films, and comparing those scenes is revealing. The bar represents community in each film, but each bar scene also depicts a degree of alienation from that community. In *Secaucus Seven*, the bar serves mainly to establish connections among the summer visitors and their townie friends, and it is also the place where the differences between these two groups becomes most clear. In *Lianna*, the bar provides the protagonist's first exposure to the lesbian community, but she does not at first feel a part of it. The bar in *Baby, It's You* represents the working-class community, from which Jill feels alienated. In each of these taverns, then, there is a sense of community against which the outsiders are defined. That pattern seems to be repeated in *Brother*, but the community that exists in Odell's seems already to be defined by a failure to communicate even before the mute alien enters (see figure 5). The regulars keep up a running commentary on the newcomer, but they talk mainly across, rather than to, each other. This almost Pinteresque dialogue continues in the bar throughout the film, regardless of who happens in. When the men in black appear, even the implicit violence of Pinter's language is suggested, though like Pinter, Sayles can turn threatening speech into humor. Thus if Odell's gives us the strongest sense of a community that we see in Harlem—the regulars will eventually come to the Brother's defense against the men in black—it is clearly a deficient community. The film itself is about why.

Among the regulars in the bar we find, of course, an alcoholic, but also a young man who seems to be addicted to the video game he's constantly playing. The machine is malfunctioning, and that gives the Brother the opportunity to come to the rescue. He fixes the machine merely by laying on his hands, rather like a faith healer for electronics. This ability will allow the Brother to find work in an arcade fixing broken machines. The fact that he works at all is itself remarkable; Hollywood's space aliens do not normally have jobs, but work is a constant in Sayles's films. The Brother's way with electronics gives him the means to

Figure 5. Bernice (Ren Woods), Odell (Steve James), Fly (Darryl Edwards), Smokey (Leonard Jackson), Walter (Bill Cobbs), and Sam (Tom Wright): the regulars at Odell's bar.

earn money, and he understands its usefulness. Unlike most Americans, however, he has no interest in the stuff for its own sake, or to have more than needed to satisfy his immediate, simple desires. Later in the film, after he is told he lacks the amount necessary to pay the cover charge at a club, he leaves what he does have on the counter.

The group at Odell's also helps the Brother find a place to stay. The key person in this effort is Sam (Tom Wright), a welfare worker who also is most important in finding the Brother a job. He knows of a woman, Randy Sue Carter (Caroline Aaron), who takes in boarders. She is white and from Alabama and has been abandoned by her African American boyfriend, leaving her with a five-year-old son and his mother to care for. This interracial family, and the multiracial staff of the welfare office represent social bonds that otherwise are lacking in Harlem. Randy Sue, who talks constantly, filling in the aural vacuum that the Brother's lack of speech creates, represents the all too familiar "broken family" associated with ghetto life. Yet she is white, and she is obviously self-reliant and caring. Meanwhile, the welfare office is depicted as hobbled by red tape, but its workers are clearly trying to help their clients. When the men in black show up looking for the Brother, Noreen (Maggie Renzi) stalls them with a myriad of bureaucratic doublespeak and requests for paper work. Rather than portraying the government agency as oppressive or incompetent, Sayles presents it as doing its job, looking out for people's welfare.

Odell's bar, Randy Sue's home, and the welfare office represent the positive, daylight side of Harlem. The film's pivotal sequence takes place, however, at night where the Brother finds himself in "Babylon." After he notices a man running away from something, the Brother goes to discover what it was and finds a girl dead of an overdose of heroin, the needle still in her arm. We might expect the Brother to try to heal her, as he was able to do with the cut on his landlady's son's leg, but instead he tastes the drug he finds in her pocket and then injects himself with what was left in the syringe. We assume the Brother's motive for taking the drug is curiosity, in that he wants to understand why the girl died. But the drug is also narratively a bit like a magic potion, because the sequence that follows gives him a new vision of the world he is visiting.

After nodding off, the Brother awakens to see a man in dreadlocks saying in Jamaican patois, "welcome to Babylon, brother." While reggae plays in the background, the man continues, "Let Virgil guide you, man, and inform you of the ways of the night." Virgil (Sidney Sheriff Jr.) then takes the Brother on a stroll through Harlem, which by allusion to Dante is Hell. The film's color scheme shifts when Virgil appears. When the Brother stumbles out of the alley where he found the dead girl, the colors are bluish and cool. But on waking up, the dominant tone is orange, imitating the color of sodium vapor lamps often used on urban streets. This unearthly lighting and the strong nighttime contrasts create a very different visual world than we find elsewhere in the film. It is as if the Brother has learned only one side of his new planet, and now he is introduced to the dark side. Like Dante's Virgil, the Brother's guide explains what is seen:

> Children withering away up here, brother, worshipping the idol of capital, lusting after the false salvation of the here and now. Black brother and sister perishing up here, man, waiting for scraps from oppressor's table. Oppressor got us a whore's bed, doing tricks to get reward. Oppressor need a slave, him find it here. Oppressor need a harlot, him find it here. Oppressor don't need you at all, him always find another man.

At this point, the two encounter several prostitutes who proposition them, and Virgil's analysis, already difficult to understand both because of his accent and the sound mixing, becomes background to their spiel. A moment later, we hear him say more clearly,

> Nighttime is promise, brother. You make deals in the night, pay all you got for what you can't see. And when the sun come up and illuminate, you been cheated again. All the people is there walking the streets at nighttime, brother. All the people feel it. People dream, people fear, people hatred. . . . We're killing each other on these streets, brother.

As we hear this part of Virgil's monologue, we see a man break dancing by himself in front of a graffiti-strewn medal shutter, as if to remind us that even in this Hell, life and art persist. Here the lighting becomes even more striking, as the dancer moves between the blue-toned shutter and the orange light closer to the street. The Brother and Virgil watch him in front of what looks like an orange fog pierced by a line of white street lamps.

The guide and his tourist end up in front of a fire in a trash barrel, where they warm themselves and Virgil offers the Brother a joint, saying "this place is not your own, brother," encouraging him to "take a ship back . . ., take a ship home to the promised land." He refuses at first, but then accepts. We see shots of people sleeping outside in easy chairs, and then of the Brother looking stoned. There's a cut to a shot of his shoeless feet sticking up in front of his supine body the next morning, the shoes that Randy Sue had given him apparently stolen. This conclusion renders Virgil an unreliable guide, and it serves to undercut any sense that his monologue was a straightforward statement of Sayles's message. When the sun has come up, the Brother too has been cheated.

Still, Virgil's tour gives us the most disturbing picture of Harlem in the film. In addition to the drug addicts and prostitutes, we see an urban landscape in decay. The episode as a whole, beginning with the discovery of the dead girl, provides the impetus for the Brother to find out who the "oppressor" really is. The Brother now has a mission to discover the source of the drug the girl died taking. Using his own removable eye like a video recorder, the Brother learns about her dealer's connections, and he traces them back to a man who lives in a suburban mansion in New Jersey. The Brother follows this drug kingpin to his office in a Manhattan high rise, and finds him bagging his product for sale. The confrontation scene is effective in part because the Brother cannot speak, making Mr. Vance (Edward Baran) do all of the talking. He tries to buy off the Brother, saying "Whoever's paying you isn't paying you for this what I could. I've got an organization here. We're diversifying. We're moving in every direction." He seems to explain the drugs as a way to raise needed cash for a business in trouble: "It solves some cash flow problems." This corporate jargon links this drug lord to the "idol of capital." He is an oppressor not merely because he is a merchant of death, but because he exploits people to acquire capital. The confrontation ends with the Brother avenging the girls' death by forcing Vance's face into a bag of heroin.

As the Brother has been chasing down the drug dealer, the men in black have been pursing him. They finally capture the Brother as he emerges from the office building. They insert some kind of electronic plug into a receptacle in the Brother's side that allows them to reel him back in when he attempts to flee. The Brother manages to knock the controller away, and to remove the device from his body. After being chased through New York streets and alleys, the Brother comes upon a group that we take to be other escapees from his planet. The men in black now become the pursued, and the group chases them into a parking lot where, surrounded, they self-destruct. The film thus concludes with Harlem fulfilling the promise suggested by the opening shot of the Statue of Liberty, but only because of the solidarity the escaped slaves have with each other. This illustrates a premise of Sayles's work: that the community makes possible the life and the liberty of the individual. Where most American cinema has insisted that individual freedom is threatened by the demands of society, Sayles repeatedly shows how without social bonds, individuals not only victimize each other, but they also must fail to achieve their own potential.

Sayles had a number of independent distributors interested in the finished film, and he went with a new company, Cinecom. *The Brother from Another Planet* opened in New York in September 1984 to a weak review from Vincent Canby in the *New York Times*, but solid box office. The film continued to do well as it opened across the country during the fall. While it never played on more than 28 screens, *Brother* ended up bringing in a higher percentage return on investment than any of Sayles's films except *Secaucus Seven*. This response happened despite reviews that were mixed at best. We begin to get criticism of Sayles as lacking in style and being too serious or moralistic, and these themes will continue to a greater or lesser degree throughout his career. Although a number of critics praise Sayles's visuals in *Brother*, Paul Attanasio in the *Washington Post* comments on Sayles's style, "all his movies are hampered by an almost shocking ignorance of filmmaking fundamentals—he just doesn't know where to put his camera." And while some critics found Sayles's treatment of race enlightening, Jay Scott in the *Toronto Globe and Mail* complains, "The Brother's crusade to rid Harlem of heroin appears to be misguided moralism."

After the release of *Brother*, Sayles directed three music videos for Bruce Springsteen for songs on the *Born in the USA* album. In 1984, MTV was only three years old, but it had had an enormous impact on the recording industry. Springsteen had not previously released many promotional videos, but Columbia felt that *Born in the USA* had a chance to be a major hit and put up the money. The video for the first released single from that album, "Dancing in the Dark," directed by Brian De Palma, was a sort of simulated concert in which a young Courtney Cox is invited up onto the stage by the Boss to dance with him. Springsteen felt that it was too slick, and asked Sayles to do something grittier.

The first video Sayles directed was for the song "Born in the USA," and it consists of concert footage edited together from three L.A. shows and documentary images shot in New Jersey that to some extent illustrate the song's lyrics. These images are used mainly during the instrumental sections of the song, while we see Springsteen sing most of the lyrics. The concert footage is striking, with much of it shot in tight focus on Springsteen's face. Dressed in a denim jacket, needing a shave, and wearing a headband holding back his almost Afro style hair, Springsteen himself certainly looks gritty, especially compared to his almost preppy appearance on the De Palma video. The video opens with a shot of an American flag, and it closes with a now famous shot of the artist's butt, as he walks away from the camera and toward a flag, the camera panning up to his head as he turns to look over his shoulder at it. These flag-filled scenes bracket a series of images of working-class life, beginning with shots of a refinery and its workers.

The video thus embodies, rather than clarifies, the contradiction central to this record. President Ronald Reagan during his 1984 reelection campaign tried to appropriate "Born in the USA," treating it as a celebration of America and therefore an endorsement of his regime. It could be misread as a celebration of America because the song sounds like an anthem and a celebration despite the very uncelebratory picture its lyrics paint:

> Born down in a dead man's town
> The first kick I took was when I hit the ground
> You end up like a dog that's been beat too much
> Till you spend half your life just covering up.

Sayles's video shows us, among other things, a line outside a check-cashing service, a hot rod with a for-sale sign, and a military graveyard, all images that underline the critique made in the songs verses. But there are more images that are neutral, like the refinery, or perhaps even positive, such as scenes from an amusement park. It is then, a faithful visual rendering of this recording, and it is another illustration of Sayles's predilection for letting audiences draw their own conclusions.

The other two videos are narratives based on stories Springsteen came up with, videos featuring the singer as an auto mechanic ("I'm On Fire") and a heavy equipment operator ("Glory Days"). These videos stand out not only from most of Springsteen's, which have typically been performance videos, but also from the dominant style of music videos in the mid-1980s. Although the music video as a genre was characterized by avant-garde strategies such as self-reflexivity and pastiche, these videos are fairly traditional. "I'm On Fire," where the auto mechanic is depicted as desiring a wealthy woman on whose car he works, contrasts the grimy, realistically presented world of the garage with both the woman, dressed in white and wearing gold jewelry, and the mechanic's nighttime trip to return her vintage Thunderbird. We see Springsteen get up out of a single bed, as he sings "At night I wake up with the sheet soaking wet." The next scenes are connected by long dissolves that make them seem dreamlike, and it is unclear whether they are meant to represent a literal dream. But when the mechanic arrives at the woman's house, shots of it and him are connected by straight cuts, as if he has come back to reality. He decides not to ring the bell but to leave the keys and walk away.

"Glory Days" is somewhat more complex because it seems to deal with three levels of reality. The video opens with a shot of Springsteen in the cab of a pile driver. The scene fades into one where we see him alone on a diamond pitching baseballs at a backstop (see figure 6). As the music begins, there is a cut to Springsteen and the E Street Band playing in a small bar. Most of the video is taken up with this performance, which is, however, intercut not only with scenes from elsewhere in the bar but also of Springsteen as the operator/pitcher watching a baseball game on television, apparently in his living room. Although one could easily read the bar scene merely as a Bruce Springsteen concert, it could also be understood as an instance of working-class leisure, putting the entire video within the experience of that class. The video concludes with the pitcher throwing to a young batter, who asks him who he pitched against today. The pitcher replies, "San Diego. Nettles got me with two out in the ninth." The exchange reveals that the equipment operator's pitching is a part of his fantasy life, corresponding to the song's lyrics about a former high-school baseball star who can't stop talking about his glory days. It is telling that even in his fantasy, he loses the game.

In this song, and on *Born in the USA* as an album, the dreams that lived in Springsteen's earlier songs no longer inspire hope, but are consigned to the past, when one was foolish enough to believe in them. There is a continuum in the video from the utterly repetitive and apparently meaningless work of running the pile driver, to the less alienated

Figure 6. Bruce Springsteen as working-class hero in "Glory Days."

but still repetitive, lonely, and unsuccessful pitching, to the unambiguous pleasure of the band as it plays. Clearly the band is enjoying its work, yet even this enjoyment is qualified by the fact that the bar patrons don't seem to be listening.

The videos for "I'm On Fire" and "Glory Days" give us a Springsteen who looks like someone from the working class, and that look became part of Springsteen's persona. Sayles's videos were a significant part of the remaking of the Boss's image, noted by *Newsweek* in a photo retrospective labeled "the five faces of Springsteen," which called him "a working-class hero" in an image from the "Glory Days" video (Barol). But the class identification solidified in these images coexists with a national identification announced in the title of the album, *Born in the USA*. The potential conflict between these two identities parallels the contradiction we noted in "Born in the USA," a conflict between upbeat, joyous music and the pointed critical social commentary of many of the lyrics. The "Glory Days" video makes this conflict more evident than does the record, because the song's lyrics don't involve the explicit critique of the album's title track. Although Sayles's films never make use of explicit patriotic imagery, they often deal with unresolved political contradictions. Sayles thus shares with Springsteen more than the geographic and class affinities displayed in these videos, but also a certain intellectual kinship.

Matewan

Sayles's next two films represent a distinctly new direction, into history. Most low-budget films, whether independent or not, are set in the present because that makes it possible to use ordinary locations, costumes, and objects as they exist when the film is being made. Hollywood over the years has made some genuinely interesting historical films (e.g., *Patton*, Franklin J. Schaffner, 1970; *Glory*, Edward Zwick, 1989), but history is usually mere backdrop for adventure or romance. Sayles, however, demonstrated with *Matewan* and *Eight Men Out* that he took the task of accurately representing the past seriously, and that convincing period re-creation could be done on budgets much lower than the studios would devote to a project with a contemporary setting. But perhaps more important, Sayles's history films show why history matters.

With *Brother* out in the theaters, Sayles returned to *Matewan*. This time, Sayles and his producers, Peggy Rajski and Maggie Renzi, were able to find money from a variety of sources. Cinecom had had success distributing films such as *Stop Making Sense* (Jonathan Demme, 1984) and *A Room with a View* (James Ivory, 1985), and it was in the position to contribute some money to the production of *Matewan*. The success of films like *A Room with a View* demonstrated to the industry the growing potential for profits from independent productions. *Matewan*, however, was not a gentle comedy of manners cast with famous British stage actors but a political film that would probably have no recognizable faces. Thus, as usual, Sayles contributed a third of the cost from his profits on *Brother* and fees from the Springsteen videos. The remainder came from individuals, including several members of the cast. The production budget came to $3.6 million, much larger than any of Sayles's previous films, but it was tiny given that the film would have a period setting and would require such expensive elements as the rental of a steam locomotive.

Sayles has told several slightly different stories about how he learned about the Matewan Massacre, the historical event on which *Matewan* is based. In *Thinking in Pictures*, his book about the making of the film, he says that it happened while researching his novel *Union Dues*, though his interest in the West Virginia coalfields stemmed from having hitchhiked through the region in the 1960s. A significant portion of the film's plot first appeared in that novel as a story told by Pappy, an old West Virginia miner, but the story is not associated there with the Matewan Massacre. Sayles reports reading about the massacre in a book about the Hatfield-McCoy feud in Mingo County, which mentioned that Police Chief Sid Hatfield, a cousin of the feuding family, had been involved in a shoot-out with company thugs. Sayles then read contemporary accounts in left-wing and union newspapers, which supported the miners, and national and local newspapers, which were antiunion. The details that all of them agreed upon he took to be the facts of the story. Elsewhere, Sayles says that "he first heard stories of the coal wars of the twenties . . . by word of mouth from coal miners and their relatives as I hitchhiked through West Virginia" (Foreword vii). Apparently, his idea for the film stemmed from these stories, which he thought had "a lot of the Old West to them" (*Thinking* 10).

The story of Matewan and the West Virginia mine war of 1920–21 has never been part of standard American history textbooks. Indeed, the history of the union movement in the United States was pretty much ignored even by professional historians until, in the wake of the 1960s revival of the American left, scholars of Sayles's generation took up the subject. Films about union struggles have also been scarce. Besides *Salt of the Earth* alluded to in *Secaucus Seven*, post-1945 films about unions include Martin Ritt's *The Molly McGuires* (1970), about a militant nineteenth-century miners union, and his contemporary drama, *Norma Rae* (1979), about organizing in a Southern textile mill. Barbara Koppel's documentary *Harlan County* (1976) concerned a contemporary coal miners strike in southeastern Kentucky, which suggests that little has changed for union organizers since the events told in *Matewan*. When Sayles was doing his research in the 1970s, there was no book-length study of the West Virginia coal war. By the time *Matewan* was beginning production, Sayles discovered *Thunder in the Mountains* by Lon Savage, the first history of the mine war. Around the time of *Matewan*'s release, Denise Giardina's novel about the war, *Storming Heaven*, appeared. Together with Sayles's film, these sources make the history of the West Virginia coalfields more available, but it's safe to say that this chapter, like the history of the labor movement in general, remains unfamiliar to most Americans.

Matewan tells the story of events leading up to and including the Matewan Massacre, in which union workers and their allies, including local lawmen, won a shoot-out with Baldwin-Felts agents hired by the mine owners. The United Mine Workers had organized a very successful recruitment campaign in southern West Virginia, and the mine owners, who fired anyone who joined the union, were desperately trying to bring it to an end. According to Savage's account, the gun battle started when Sid Hatfield and Matewan Mayor C. C. Testerman attempted to arrest Baldwin-Felts detectives who had been illegally evicting striking miners and their families. No one knows who fired the first shot, but in the end seven detectives, including two Felts brothers, two miners, and Mayor Testerman were killed. Sid Hatfield became a hero to miners throughout the nation, as someone who had finally "stood up to the hated Baldwin-Felts detectives. For twenty years these extralegal strike-breaking guns-for-hire had harassed union miners all over the country. Stories of their atrocities were told in every miner's cabin: it was Baldwin-Feltses who burned women and children at Ludlow in Colorado; Baldwin-Feltses tracked down miners with bloodhounds and throwed 'em in jail; 'Baldwins' forced little children from their homes at gunpoint; Baldwins machine-gunned sleeping miners at Holly Grove" (Savage 25). This history grounds Sayles's depiction of the Baldwin-Felts agents, but he did not include the worst of their atrocities.

Focusing on union organizing and the working class, *Matewan* is Sayles's most traditionally left-wing film. Sayles tells the story from the miners' point of view, and he chooses to emphasize the value and valor of their struggle. Yet, Sayles is a man of the 1960s, not of the 1930s, and *Matewan* is not mainly concerned with demonstrating the miners' case. Rather, its focus is an issue proper to the Civil Rights Movement and to the New Left, the question of violence as a political strategy. Violence was used by both the owners and the miners of the era, with the owners finally winning the war only after the federal government sent in troops and even airplanes to quash the rebellion. Sayles says, "the first major decision I made in writing *Matewan* was to not just pick a side and root for that side to be left standing when the smoke cleared, but to question the violence itself, to question it politically, strategically, morally" (*Thinking* 16).

Yet it is important to understand that Sayles was not trying to make a docudrama nor a historical documentary. In addition to making many small changes, often done to make the film more representative of the larger struggle, *Matewan* takes its basic structure from Westerns such as *Shane* (George Stevens, 1953) and *High Noon* (Fred Zinneman, 1952). It begins with the appearance of a stranger in town, union organizer Joe Kenehan (Chris Cooper) (see figure 7), closely followed by the arrival of the bad guys dressed in black, Baldwin-Felts agents Hickey (Kevin Tighe) and Griggs (Gordon Clapp). The kerosene lighting, clothing styles, and other visual cues also make us think of the Old West. Music, as in many Westerns, sometimes moves into the foreground, and the Appalachian tunes and instruments would be appropriate in them. The film ends with a shoot-out in the single main street of the town of Matewan, with the police chief and mayor facing the Baldwin-Felts agents in the manner of the traditional Western gunfight. In its most basic form, then, the political conflict Sayles depicts in *Matewan* is not meant to be ambiguous, relative, or ironic. In keeping with traditional Westerns,

Figure 7. A stranger, Joe Kenehan (Chris Cooper), arrives in Matewan.

the identification of good and evil is obvious. Although these familiar devices might have been expected to help make the film attractive to a broad audience, they may also have put off critics and others who failed to recognize that Sayles was adapting them to a new purpose.

We are able to discuss John Sayles's intentions in *Matewan* with an unusual degree of specificity because *Thinking in Pictures* is a book about the making of the film. There he acknowledges, "The plot and structure of the Matewan story resemble the classic American Western so closely that the movie is going to automatically evoke a whole lifetime of movies that play by certain rules, that maintain certain codes" (16). Yet Sayles claims that he is not repeating those rules and codes, but calling them into question. Joe reminds viewers of Western heroes such as Alan Ladd's title role in *Shane* or Jimmy Stewart's Ransom Stoddard in *The Man Who Shot Liberty Valance* (John Ford, 1962), who seek to live peaceably but who find they must resort to violence to defend the community. But Kenehan is a pacifist and will not strap on a gun at the end of the film. The law is often depicted as ineffectual in a Western, but the sheriff or marshal is typically one of its heroes. *Matewan* follows this convention via the character of Sid Hatfield (David Strathairn), who has the courage to confront the Baldwin-Felts despite their ruthlessness and their working for the mine owners. Yet, unlike in the typical Western, Sid is a marginal character.

In Sayles's conception, then, *Matewan* is a bent Western, which would seem to indicate similarities to such films as *Butch Cassidy and the Sundance Kid* (George Roy Hill, 1969) and *McCabe and Mrs. Miller* (Robert Altman, 1971). Yet those movies are always perceived as bending genre rules, while *Matewan* generally has not been. The Western is a mythic genre, one not usually associated with realism. In borrowing from the Western and in choosing a period setting, Sayles consciously moves away from the realism of his first films, but he hardly abandons it completely. The film claims to tell the truth about the events and about their social context—the workers' living conditions, their economic situation, etc. But it also seeks to elevate the struggle it depicts, treating it as both unusually heroic and symbolic of the struggles of labor as a whole. Thus, one difficulty in reading the film arises from crossing a mythic genre in which the opposing sides were by convention uncontroversial with the social problem picture, a genre committed to realism. Many assume that realism must entail an attempt at balance, that the point of view of both sides will be revealed, even if the film in the end comes down on one side or the other. For Sayles, the problem is one of the role of violence in political struggles and his approach to that is balanced; that the workers' struggle is righteous, he has no doubt.

The question of violence is thematized throughout the film, both visually and in dialogue. It's already implicit in the film's opening scene, where we see miners discussing the company's reduction in their pay, just before a charge one of them has planted goes off. The use of violence by the miners is introduced at the first union meeting that Kenehan attends in Matewan. A miner says, "the first thing we got to have is alla these niggers and alla these dagoes that come here to take our jobs thrown out of the mines." C. E. Lively (a historical figure later revealed to be a company spy, played by Bob Gunton) asserts that the only thing the coal operators and their gun thugs "understand is the bad end of a bullet. And if we show 'em we'd just as soon blow up their damn mines as see 'em worked by a bunch of scabs, then they're gonna listen." The meeting allows Sayles to set up both the question of violence and another of the film's chief concerns, the way in which the ruling class used race and ethnicity as wedges that would divide workers. When a black worker, Few Clothes (James Earl Jones) shows up at the meeting, he is brought in at gunpoint and called a scab. Kenehan then speaks up for the first time: "Union men, my ass!" He walks to the center of the room, and the camera follows him. Pointing to Few Clothes, he continues, "You think this man is your enemy? Huh? This is a worker! Any union keeps this man out ain't a union it's a goddam club! They got you fightin' white against colored, native against foreign, hollow against hollow, when you know there ain't but two sides in this world—them that work and them that don't. You work, they don't. That's all you got to know about the enemy." As he speaks, there are occasional cuts to the faces of C.E. and the miners, who appear unconvinced. Kenehan moves among the miners, and continues, "You say you've got guns." He pauses, and there's a cut to C.E. Kenehan resumes,

> Well I know that you're all brave men, and I know you could shoot it out with the company if you had to. But the coal company don't want this union, the state government don't want it, the federal government don't want it and they're all of 'em just waitin' for an excuse to come down and crush us to nothing. Fellas, we're in a hole full of coal gas here. The tiniest spark at the wrong time is going to be the end of us. So we got to pick away at this situation slow and careful. We got to organize and build support. We got to work together—together—till they can't get their coal out of the ground without us cause we're a union, cause we're the workers dammit and we take care of each other!

The scene contains little in the way of action. It occurs in a small space with workers more or less crammed in. Kenehan, an outsider, makes himself the center of attention, and Chris Cooper's performance compels the attention of the audience as well. The film has already set us up to identify with Kenehan, and here his powerful articulation of the principles of solidarity in the face of skepticism and outright hostility make him seem like a natural leader. Kenehan's speech is contrasted with those of the Hardshell Preacher (John Sayles) and of Danny (Will Oldham), who are both preaching at a church service while the union meeting is in progress. Sayles cuts between the two events, first giving us the Hardshell Preacher's antiunion sermon, and then, following the union meeting, Danny's prounion interpretation of the parable of the workers in the vineyard. While these two sermons serve to reinforce our sympathy with the union side, and to make the antiunion position seem irrational and perhaps even Satanic by virtue of Sayles's portrayal of the character, neither address the worker's immediate needs and interests the way Kenehan does. But, he is also presented as having convictions that are as strong and at least as worthy as those of the preachers. We are convinced that he believes deeply in what he is saying, and we are meant to feel his persuasive power—as opposed to the Hardshell Preacher's mere stirring of emotions or Danny's storytelling. Kenehan's speech establishes both what the film will henceforth take for granted—that the world is divided into two opposing classes—and what it will put up for debate: violence versus nonviolence as a strategy in the class war.

Kenehan's opposition to violence is contrasted not only with the miners' willingness to use it, but also with the love of violence evidenced in Baldwin-Felts thugs, Hickey (Kevin Tighe) and Griggs (Gordon Clapp). C.E. is shown writing to the agency to send help after he sees Kenehan in action, and Hickey and Griggs show up in Matewan as a result. Hickey comes off as a sadist from his first scene where he calls Bridey May (Nancy Mette), the first person he meets in Matewan, "a piece of mountain trash." He clearly relishes violence, and later in the film tells a story about how he bayoneted a German soldier after he came into his trench during the war. Hickey was called a war hero for this, but he tells the story to make it clear that killing was something he enjoyed. Thus, Hickey reminds us of the hired gun Jack Wilson (Jack Palance) in *Shane*, or of any number of roles played by Lee Marvin, including Liberty Valance. Since the mine owners do not really figure in the film, Hickey and Griggs, along with the spy, C.E., are *Matewan*'s main villains. But it's not just, or perhaps even mainly, the side of capital for which they stand; Hickey especially represents violence itself. That's why Hickey is Kenehan's most prominent opponent.

Hickey and Grigg's nastiness is on display not only in their work—threatening and harassing the strikers—but also in their manners. After insulting Bridey May, they head for Elma's boarding house, where Kenehan has been staying. First her son Danny, then Elma (Mary McDonnell), tell them that there is no vacancy, but the men insist threateningly, saying that the Stone Mountain Coal Company owns the house, and they are working for the company. Whereas earlier we had seen Joe at the dinner table with the family acting well-mannered and interested in their lives, Hickey and Griggs are demanding, insulting, and otherwise boorish. Later in the film, they bring a bottle of whiskey to the table and mock the family's religious beliefs. In a sense, the family members are their hostages, and they treat them as such.

In his speech at the union meeting, nonviolence is presented only as strategy, and Kenehan makes no attempt to persuade his audience that there might be larger reasons to eschew violence. Later in the film, however, his pacifism is spelled out. Kenehan has been set up by C.E., who uses his friendship with Bridey May, a young widow, to get the miners to believe that the union organizer is the company spy. The men draw straws to see who should kill Kenehan, and Few Clothes gets the short one. He sits down by Joe in the strikers' camp, holstering a six-gun and telling him that he is there to protect him from a rumored attack by the Baldwins. Most of the miners are off listening to Danny preach so that they will have an alibi. Danny, who knows that Joe has been framed, but can't openly reveal his knowledge because Hickey and Griggs are there to keep an eye on him, revises the Old Testament story of Joseph and Potiphar's wife to let the other miners know the truth. Intercut with Danny's sermon, Joe explains to Few Clothes why he doesn't carry a gun. He tells a long story about some Mennonites whom he observed while serving time in Leavenworth. They were in prison for refusing to serve in World War I, and they went on strike to protest being forced to shave and wear uniforms with buttons, both of which were against their religion. Even after being tortured, they refused to yield. Kenehan makes the lesson clear: "them fellas, never lifted a gun in their lives, you couldn't find any braver in my book." The story has no plot significance, but it makes clear Joe's commitment to pacifism, which is rendered heroic in his story. Meanwhile, Danny's message is understood by the miners, and they send someone to call off the killing in the nick of time, rendering Danny the real hero of this sequence. That is important, because Danny, as an old man, will turn out to be the narrator of the film, the one who will in the future preach union and nonviolence.

With C.E. exposed—he swims away to Kentucky to avoid the miners' wrath—and Kenehan vindicated, the strike becomes increasingly successful. That makes the owners all the more determined to break the strike. Hickey, having been unable to bribe Sid Hatfield, has more

Baldwin-Felts agents sent to town to enforce evictions and arrest the police chief if he stands in their way. This sets up the final showdown. The sequence begins with Fausto (Joe Gifasi) coming to tell Joe that the men have gone to town. We then shift to a shot of the town, where a flock of birds scatters from a roof-top roost. Sid is waiting on a bench, when Mayor Testerman (Josh Mostel) arrives. Sid tells him he doesn't need to be there, but the mayor replies that it's his town, too. As we see a large group of Baldwin-Felts men walking up the railroad tracks toward the officials, Sid opens his suit coat to reveal a six-gun on each side of him, but the Mayor is apparently unarmed (see figure 8). There are repeated

Figure 8. The show-down in Matewan: Sid Hatfield (David Strathairn) faces the Baldwin-Felts thugs.

shot/reverse shot alterations, familiar from Western showdowns. When the two lead agents come within a few feet, there is a moment of tense silence. The Mayor begins to tell the agents that they have no right to be there, and there is a cut to Kenehan running into the scene behind him. One of the agents draws his shoulder-holstered gun, and then we cut to Joe yelling "no," and back to Sid as he draws both of his guns. Shots ring out as the Mayor falls, echoing Joe with a cry of "no," and Sid shoots the two lead agents at point-blank range. It is impossible to know who fired first. We then see the miners, who have been hidden from view, firing at the main body of agents, who return fire and scatter. The battle rages until the Baldwin-Felts men have been driven out of the center of town. There are numerous images of both agents and miners getting shot.

The scene shifts to the steps of Elma's boarding house, where we see Hickey wounded in the leg trying to escape the battle. He climbs up and walks behind a line of bed linens hanging to dry and turns to face the street, all but his head hidden. He notices a miner who doesn't see him and raises his pistol. But he hears the sound of a gun being cocked behind him, and he turns to see Elma, most of her body hidden behind a sheet. He raises his hands with a big grin on his face, and she fires her shotgun into his gut, blood covering the hanging laundry. She fires the second barrel for good measure, her face suggesting satisfaction at finishing off this monster. There's a cut to a young Baldwin-Felts agent running toward the camera. We have learned earlier that he had been duped by a want ad and didn't know what he was getting into. Now he encounters Danny training his Springfield rifle on him, and he pleads, "Jesus, don't shoot me." After holding the rifle on him for a bit, Danny lowers it, and the agent runs past him into the river to make his escape.

This sequence, which could be called a kind of coda to the massacre scene, illustrates the ambiguity of the film's ending. On the one hand, Elma's shooting of Hickey is deeply satisfying. He has been the most sadistic of the thugs, and, perhaps worse, a bad guest in Elma's house. Moreover, at the moment of his death, he believes he is safe because a woman is holding the gun. *Matewan*, unlike Sayles's previous films, is not much about women, who are mainly part of the background of this story. But having a woman kill "Liberty Valance," is a reversal typical of Sayles's feminism. Following this scene with Danny sparing the young agent, however, makes it clear Sayles will not allow revenge to stand unquestioned. Of course, the man Danny spares has done nothing but choose the wrong side, but we get the sense that most of the other miners would not have been so forgiving. The incident shows us that Danny is special, a Christian who shows mercy, a union man who recognizes that an individual worker like this agent is not his real enemy. At this point, the battle seems to have been a triumph for the good guys.

That changes in light of the next sequence, which takes place back in the center of town. We see Sid checking the bodies of the dead Baldwins. Mayor Testerman is seen sitting up holding his belly, complaining that he can't feel his legs. Hillard's mother is seen emptying a revolver into the dead Griggs. Then we see first Elma and then Danny, still carrying their weapons, staring at something on the tracks. There's a cut to Joe Kenehan lying dead across the rails, as Elma kneels beside him and breaks down. Her tears imply a romance that might have been, one that Sayles, following Western convention, elected not to develop.

There's a cut back to a medium close shot of Danny, and we hear the beginning of the film's voice-over epilogue. It tells the rest of the story of the massacre and the coal war, how Sid was gunned down unarmed by Baldwin-Felts agents on the steps of the McDowell County Courthouse, with C. E. Lively finishing him off with a shot in the head, and that no one was even tried for Sid's murder. We hear that the miners took the worst of it in the war, just as Joe said they would, and Pappy reports that after the Matewan Massacre, he preached that it was "one big union the world over. . . . That was my religion." As the voice-over ends, we see Danny coming out of a mine, his face blackened, and realize that he has been the film's narrator.

The end of *Matewan* reports the failure of armed resistance as a strategy, but it does not suggest that nonviolence would have won the day for the miners. It is clear that the thugs whom the mine owners hired were more than willing to kill unarmed men and women. The resistance of the miners is presented as a failure, but a heroic one nevertheless. As Sayles put it, "the psychological victory of those violent days may have been more important" than the miners' defeat at Blair Mountain. "when a colonized people learn they can fight back together, life can never again be so comfortable for their exploiters" (Foreword viii). We feel both encouraged by the miners' resistance, and cautioned that resistance, violent or nonviolent, does not always produce change.

Matewan shows that Sayles has mastered his craft in all of its facets. It is his first film where one does not see evidence of budgetary limitations, something all the more remarkable because of the period setting. Some of this has to do with having access to better talent, both in front of and behind the camera. Haskell Wexler, who had previously won an Oscar for *Bound for Glory*, was nominated for cinematography for this film, the first nomination for a Sayles film. Much of the film was shot in low-light conditions, under which Wexler was able to create sufficient clarity without sacrificing the dark look such scenes needed. Even full-daylight scenes have a somewhat subdued tone, without ever seeming to be in sepia. The professional look of the film benefited enormously from the work of production designer Nora Chavooshian, art director Dan Bishop (who would go on to be production designer on the TV series *Mad Men*), and costume designer, Cynthia Flint, who found most of the wardrobe in West Virginia thrift stores. The acting benefited from the maturation of Sayles's ensemble players, especially David Strathairn. But more important, Chris Cooper and Mary McDonnell, both appearing in their first feature film, created subtle and compelling characters in performances unlike any Sayles had previously directed. James Earl Jones brought a gravitas to the film that it's hard to imagine any other actor of the period contributing.

It is something of a conundrum then that the reviews for *Matewan* were mostly negative. Indeed, only Vincent Canby seems to have understood the complexity of Sayles's vision in giving the film its one rave. Although Wexler's cinematography is universally praised, as is the film's re-creation of the period, the story is often called contrived and clichéd. The tone of the negative reviews is illustrated by Rita Kempley in the *Washington Post*, who begins her pan, "It's really no surprise when John Sayles shows up as a preacher in *Matewan*." In these reviews, we begin to get criticism of Sayles that will be repeated often. For example, Peter Keough of the *Chicago Sun-Times* complained of the director's "earnestness." The film's explicitly prounion stance led some reviewers to regard it as preachy. A review in the *Village Voice* (an organ one might expect to be friendly to Sayles's politics) called *Matewan* a "'union snooze,' full of ideological pieties, improbable heroes and 'hissable villains'" (Quoted in John Williams). Kempley found it incredible that the good guys could be so good and the bad guys so bad. The implication of all of these complaints is that formal features of this film, or sometimes the director's technique, rather than the political position it stakes out, are at fault. These critics' responses suggest that any film with an explicit political position counter to the dominant one is likely to be regarded as "didactic." As viewers of Westerns, we do not complain that Liberty Valance is a "hissable villain" or that Jack Palance's gunslinger in *Shane* is "so evil." We understand that the evil they represent is not meant to be specific, and our concern is about how the hero will respond. But because the struggle between workers and capitalists continues to this day, we do not perceive those positions as conventional.

Sayles might have been able to count on an acceptance of his positioning of the good guys and bad guys had the history on which *Matewan* is based been better known. Anyone familiar with the history would have a hard time saying that Sayles distorted it. And then there's the general problem that most viewers don't even have enough historical sense to put the story in a larger context. It should be shocking to learn that in 1920—the year in which DeMille released *Why Change Your Wife?*, F. Scott Fitzgerald published *This Side of Paradise*, and women got the right to vote—that such outrages will still be perpetrated in America. The film reveals in detail the evils of the coal companies, who first swindled the workers out of their land (or simply stole it), and then confined them to virtual peonage in company towns. Because labor was so cheap and the miners had no legal recourse, they operated the mines without regard for worker safety. Because mines elsewhere in the United States were unionized, mine operators in southern West Virginia and eastern Kentucky had a competitive advantage that they were willing to go to extremes to protect. The story of the Matewan Massacre is notable because the town authorities were not corrupted by the mine owners. The fact that the story is not well known is no coincidence, however. Not only is labor history in general not taught in schools, but the one previous movie about the incident, *Smilin' Sid*, produced by the United Mine Workers shortly after the events, is lost; the only known print was stolen by coal company agents.

Another difficulty may have to do with the structure of the scene that depicts the concluding gunfight. Perhaps for reasons of historical accuracy, or perhaps because it would be too obvious, Joe Kenehan does not play the expected role of mediator. In terms of both genre and allegory, he should have been positioned between the two sides. Instead, his late arrival to the confrontation seems to inadvertently set off the shooting, and thus his death seems more ironic than tragic. Sayles thus does not take the opportunity here to restage a debate about violence, but rather allows it to take its perhaps inevitable course.

It is misleading, then, to describe Sayles's film as didactic, because that implies exactly the kind of rigid prescription for society typically associated with left-wing art of the 1930s. *Matewan*, like many of his other films, presents social problems for which solutions are not only not overtly urged, but which may not be available given the conditions and constraints depicted. It is often asserted that the typical studio-era Hollywood film begins with a social problem and then substitutes by sleight of hand a solution to a different, often purely individual one. Sayles might be said to do the opposite: to use an individual's story to illuminate a social problem. Sayles does not tell stories that by their very structure entail a solution; even when genre conventions demand such closure, Sayles often fails to provide it.

Indeed, this openness is, I suspect, exactly what earned Sayles the wrath of historian Stephen Brier, who attacked *Matewan* in *Radical History Review* for what he calls its lack of authenticity and its "truth status." The issue for Brier is not historical detail, which he concedes that Sayles largely gets right, but rather "a larger historical truth," which I think for Brier is summarized in the sentence, "*Matewan* also lacks any sense of capitalism as a system" (123).[4] In other words, in Brier's view Sayles has not presented a social totality. Brier wants, I suspect, Sayles to point toward that ultimate solution, the revolution. But this is where Sayles deviates from traditional left-wing assumptions. His view of the world might be said to be more Foucauldian than Marxian, because power is not located for him in a sovereign state that may be seized. Indeed, several of Sayles's films reveal the difficulty that people with good intentions have when they are in nominal positions of power, among them, of course, Sid Hatfield. Moreover, like Foucault, Sayles is suspicious of the very idea of a totality. His films give us differing perspectives on a world that can never be viewed at once whole.

Perhaps not surprisingly, given the negative notices, *Matewan* was not a financial success. Its gross of $1.6 million didn't cover even half of production costs. Sayles's didn't blame the reviews for this, but rather distribution challenges, partly resulting from the growth of the independent film movement. *Matewan* had to compete with many other independent films, among them *Maurice* (James Ivory, 1987) and *Hope and Glory* (John Boorman, 1987): "We didn't have time to get out word of mouth," he says. "We were yanked from some theaters in the third week when we were still doing good business" (Mitchell).

Eight Men Out

Luckily, Sayles didn't need a good showing from *Matewan* to make his next film, *Eight Men Out*, since a distribution deal for that film had already been made with Orion Pictures. Orion was an independent production company, formed in 1978 by United Artists executives who left that company in a dispute with its owner, Transamerica. While it has been referred to as a "mini-major"—it was the box-office leader during the first half of 1987—it was considered a "sanctuary for creative filmmakers," its roster including Woody Allen and Milos Forman.

Producers Midge Sandford and Sarah Pillsbury had an option on Eliot Asinof's book on which Sayles had based his screenplay. Sandford-Pillsbury hired Sayles to direct his script, and then the project was pitched to Orion. The option came due before they were ready to make the film, so Sayles ended up buying out the rights. Despite Orion's participation, Sayles and Sanford-Pillsbury Productions still had to raise money for the film, and Orion demanded only script approval, some input on casting, and that Sayles would deliver a film of less than two hours. Sayles retained the final cut, and thus had much more freedom than he did on *Baby It's You*, which had been produced by the major, Paramount. The deal with Orion gave Sayles a $6 million production budget, his largest to date. The money was necessary given the large cast, and the need to re-create a historical setting that was even more complex than *Matewan*'s.

Sayles's interest in history has rarely if ever been equaled among American filmmakers. Of his first four original screenplays, two were historical, *Matewan* and his next film *Eight Men Out*, which was actually the first script he showed to an agent. But, it's not so much making of period films that demonstrates his interest in history, but rather his attitude toward it as expressed both in those films and in print. His sense of historical complexity is revealed in interviews with the eminent historians Eric Foner and Howard Zinn. These interviews show not only that Sayles knows a great deal about history, but also that he has thought about it both as a subject and as a process. It is ironic, then, that he has often been accused of getting history wrong, when he clearly has unusually deep knowledge of it. Hollywood has almost always treated history as mere background for an individual's story, and its films have consistently oversimplified the past. Sayles is aware that a movie cannot display history in all its complexity, but he has tried to represent some of it.

If *Matewan* brought to life an event most people had not heard of, *Eight Men Out* re-creates one they thought they knew all about, but didn't. The Black Sox scandal of 1919, in which some members of the 1919 Chicago White Sox threw the World Series in return for payments from gamblers, has become part of American folklore. The event is referred to in Fitzgerald's *The Great Gatsby*, where a character named Meyer Wolfsheim is said to have fixed the series. Many people might have been aware that Wolfsheim was very loosely based on a New York gangster named Arnold Rothstein, also the basis for a Damon Runyon character, The Brain. Shoeless Joe Jackson was certainly the most famous player involved in the scandal, and many viewers would have known that he was a great hitter who was banned from baseball in his prime. He would be a character in Phil Robinson's *Field of Dreams* the next year, though only as a ghost. Neither Robinson's film nor Fitzgerald's novel tells us anything about why the players might have been willing to go along with such a scheme, or that some of them actually initiated it. Most people didn't know how strongly gambling and baseball were connected during this era, or how little Rothstein was actually in control of the plan. They also didn't know that Charles Comiskey, owner of the White Sox, paid his championship team less than the league average, a fact that gave his players not only a greater need for the gamblers' money, but also the motive of revenge.

Sayles clearly wanted to make a point of that complexity, which the film presents enough of to make it hard to follow on one viewing. The film lacks the usual Hollywood treatment of such capers, as none of the characters qualifies as a "mastermind" of the swindle, and, indeed, there is no single protagonist. The closest the film comes to having one is Buck Weaver (John Cusack), the Sox third-baseman, and the only character who we routinely see outside of the stadium or in meetings of the conspirators. His repeated conversations with a couple of newsboys allow us to hear his reflection on the events and to give us a sense of the importance of baseball to many naive but devoted fans. Sayles may have chosen Weaver for this role because, although he was privy to the players' plans to throw the series, he did not participate in them. That makes Weaver the perfect character for Sayles, someone who straddles the lines between good and evil, outside and inside. Moreover, it makes him the most sympathetic of the players, and Sayles wants us to have some sympathy for them all. But Weaver doesn't have enough screen time to become a consistent point of identification, and the film thus refuses the viewer that pleasure, making it hard to know even whom to care about. Unlike *Matewan*, then, *Eight Men Out* is not made in the form of a familiar genre; the story is emplotted as a tragedy, but it presents itself as history.

The film opens with shots of a poorer neighborhood of Chicago—the film was shot in Chicago, Cincinnati, and Indianapolis, where Bush Stadium doubled as both Comiskey Park and Cincinnati's Redland Field. More than in *Matewan*, the lighting suggests the look of old photographs. An old car, low, brick buildings, and period clothes also make it clear that we are watching a much earlier time. The look of the film is convincing, but partly because we are not meant to be looking at the lives of the wealthy, it does not give the impression of a slick surface, as has been alleged of *Chinatown* (Roman Polanski, 1974) and *Quiz Show* (Robert Redford, 1994). Perhaps because of the lack of funds to re-create the past on sets, the actual locations have the look of ordinary, lived-in spaces. Sayles paid particular attention to the baseball details, researching the matter at the Baseball Hall of Fame. The uniforms were accurate reproductions, and most of the equipment was genuine, giving the baseball scenes a distinctive look.

The tiny gloves that the players used make their fielding skills seem all the more remarkable. Sayles actually had the actors practice for two weeks prior to the start of shooting in order to be able to pass as ballplayers. The baseball scenes, as a result, are convincing, though some of the actors were clearly better athletes than others. John Cusack makes a diving catch at third base, for example, that is good enough to make a highlight reel. The game scenes were shot under much less than ideal conditions, as a lack of extras meant that narrow angles needed to be used in order not to show a mostly empty stadium. That problem does give these scenes a somewhat fragmented look, especially since viewers are used to television coverage with its constant cutting from scenes of a whole field to closer shots of particular plays. The games also are reduced to representative plays or moments, and lack any sense of the leisurely tempo of baseball, though this helps to make the film more visually engaging. Instead of the frequent moments of waiting typical of the game, we get almost constant movement.

In the opening scene, we see two boys, excited by having come up with a few coins to buy bleacher seats, heading to the ballpark to watch the White Sox. They represent an innocent love of the game and belief in its players as genuine heroes. We briefly see some of these players on the field living up to the kids' faith in them, but we then move to the press box, where Hugh Fullerton (Studs Turkel) and Ring Lardner (John Sayles) are also appreciative of the teams' ability. Someone announces that the owner is pouring in the lounge, and Ring comments, "Sports writers of the world unite. You have nothing to lose but your bar privileges." Charles Comiskey (Clifton James) enters the press box, bragging about his team. He leads the writers back into a sumptuously appointed room spread with food and drink. He continues to brag, asserting that his club is a unified team, while Sayles shows us the players on the field making an impressive double play and then feuding among themselves as they walk off the field. Comiskey is asked by a reporter about the 3–1 odds in favor of the White Sox in the upcoming World Series, and he responds, "They are underestimating us. Any bet against my Sox this series is a sucker bet. Of course, I'm not a gambling man." The last sentence is greeted with laughter from the writers. Thus gambling is shown to be an accepted part of the game, and the owner is shown to be out of touch with his team.

Sayles cuts back to the stands, where we hear Sleepy Bill Burns (Christopher Lloyd) and Bill Maharg (Richard Edson), evaluating each player's likely willingness to do business with them. Their conversation continues as Sayles cuts back and forth from them to the named players on the field, and to Comiskey's commentary on his team members to the sports writers. The sequence introduces the players to us and reveals more of the dissension among them. Because the uniforms have neither numbers nor names, it is hard to remember which is which. Sayles reintroduces most of the players more than once, but the large cast of characters—there are at least eleven White Sox players who figure significantly in the plot, plus five gamblers, three members of the Sox management, and, later, assorted lawyers, baseball officials, and others involved in the trial—makes us wish we had a scorecard. We expect that this opening sequence will give way to a focus on a few individuals, but it does not. The opening sequence, however, gives us the sense that the "national pastime" is rife with schemers of various sorts. Comiskey is reported not to pay his players "a living wage," first-baseman Chick Gandil (Michael Rooker) is called a "sport" by the gamblers, suggesting that he has already been in league with them, and even the newsboys scam an adult patron by pretending that he has spilled the younger boy's Crackerjacks.

The players leave the field, walk down into the stadium, and find a table of champagne bottles waiting for them, courtesy of Comiskey. They express approval of the gesture, but Eddie Cicotte (David Strathairn) asks when they might receive the bonuses they had been promised for winning the American League pennant. They are told that the champagne is their bonus and then discover that it is flat. Having established the players' grievances with the owner, Sayles takes us to the bar where most of the players are drinking, the sports writers are keeping an eye on them, and the gamblers are making connections (see figure 9). The bar features a woman singing Bessie Smith–style blues, and the scene is perhaps the strongest representation of the period outside of a baseball stadium. While, as we have noted, bar scenes are obligatory in a Sayles film, this one is less about community than about cliques. By who is sitting with whom, we get a sense of the different and sometimes opposing groups into which the White Sox divide.

The bar scene also gives Sayles a chance to show how the fix was initiated. In addition to Burns and Maharg, we see Joseph "Sport" Sullivan (Kevin Tighe), who is sitting in a booth with Gandil. Gandil first tells a story about a boxing match he won, but should have thrown, and then we hear him tell Sullivan how a baseball game might be fixed. Only then does the gambler ask, "what about the Sox?" Gandil says it would take $10,000 apiece for seven players, and Sullivan insists he can raise the money. The film thus suggests that Gandil actually proposes the idea

Figure 9. Hugh Fullerton (Studs Turkel) and Ring Lardner (John Sayles) in the bar.

of the fix. Before the scene is over, Gandil and Swede Risberg (Don Harvey) are approached by Burns and Maharg, and we learn that two separate groups are interested in fixing the series and that the players hope to get paid by both of them. What we also see is that the scheme is not very well organized, the players not knowing even whether they are to throw the whole series or just a couple of games.

While Sullivan claimed he could put up enough money to meet Gandil's demand, he was planning all along to ask Arnold Rothstein to put up the money. So, as it turns out, were Burns and Maharg, who approach Rothstein through an ex-boxer, Abe Attell (Michael Mantell), a member of his entourage. Both Attell and Sullivan bring the idea of fixing the series to Rothstein. He tells the boxer that he's not interested, but tells Sullivan he is. Attell, however, decides to go ahead on his own, and Sayles shows him using his role as a Rothstein enforcer to come up with some cash to begin the scam. He pays Burns and Maharg, and Rothstein has $80,000 cash delivered to Sullivan, and all of the gamblers use a substantial portion of the money to bet on the Cincinnati Reds. The players, then, despite seeming to scam the gamblers, do not get anything like the $10,000 each they expected. Only the pitcher Cicotte, who demanded his share in advance before he would participate, actually receives the ten grand.

After the first two games, which the White Sox lose, Sayles stages a brilliant sequence in a hotel corridor, where most of those involved in the scam, knowingly or not, walk past each other without realizing it. Composed of two long takes in the corridor separated by a scene in Attell's room, we get a picture here of the inability of the gamblers to manage the conspiracy, and of major league baseball to respond to it. The sequence begins when the Sox manager, Kid Gleason (John Mahoney) knocks on Comiskey's door, finding the owner already in his pajamas, and is admitted. The camera pans right to reveal Risberg walking toward us and then around a corner to knock on Gandil's door. As that door is closing, the camera pans back slightly left and tracks Comiskey and Gleason from behind as they walk down that hall, the latter muttering that "they damn well better do something." They pass Burns and Maharg, who walk toward us, the camera reversing its movement. The two gamblers knock on a door that is opened by Attell.

There's a cut to a man, seemingly the one we saw in the hall at the beginning of the scene, sitting on a bed counting cash. Attell asks the visitors what they want, and they ask for the rest of the player's share. Attell claims its all out on bets, a lie hard to maintain when the bed is covered in money. He ends up giving Burns a mere $10,000, and says that's the last they will get. The interview ends with Attell insisting that the players "make it look good tomorrow." Back out in the corridor, the second long take begins with the reverse of the action before we entered Attell's room, Burns and Maharg walking away from us, and Comiskey, Gleason, and another man walking toward us. They knock on a door on our left, and Gleason is left standing in the hall as the other two enter. The camera pans to the right showing Attell's man leaving the room, and then pans back to the left as Comiskey and the other man leave without speaking to Gleason, the room's resident, shouting after the owner "that's the whelp of a beaten cur." Finally, Risberg passes Gleason and says an awkward hello to his manager, who just stares back in response.

This sequence sets up both the failure of the scheme to provide the cash that the players expected and the beginning of what would be the failure of baseball to deal with scandal. The dim hotel corridor peopled with furtive-looking men is a perfect visual embodiment of the idea of conspiracy. The sequence economically and elegantly conveys a great deal of information, and yet the viewer who does not have benefit of a recent reading of Asinof's book may not have enough information to understand the plot points presented. For example, the identities of the men Comiskey meets with—John Heydler, president of the National League, and Ban Johnson, president of the American League—are significant; that Comiskey talked to Heydler first, despite his being in the other league, because of a long-standing feud with Johnson. That feud accounted for Johnson's unwillingness to help Comiskey, and it would have a major impact on the way in which the series-fixing was investigated and prosecuted. Asinof was able to make a genuine page-turner out of this material, but Sayles had to tell the same story in a mere two hours instead of three hundred pages. In a microcosm, then, this sequence reveals *Eight Men Out*'s strengths and weaknesses. The film is consistently visually engaging and often exciting, and it manages to be so without oversimplifying events. Yet, in not simplifying, the film fails to engage us narratively and therefore it does not help viewers develop a strong emotional investment in the story or the characters.

As Attell revealed, the gamblers believed that the White Sox would dump Game Three also, but it was never clearly part of the plan. A major problem is that the Sox pitcher for that game, Dickie Kerr (Jace Alexander), was not on the take. He pitched a shutout, and it is unclear whether the conspiring players could have thrown the game if they had tried. What Sayles suggests is that most played the game to win. Ironically, however, because the gamblers had the bet on the Reds, they were now unable to pay the players any more money. Cicotte pitching Game Four had a reason to keep to his commitment, and Sayles shows how he throws the game in one bad inning. Down four games to one in a best of nine series, the White Sox win the next two, pitched by Kerr and Cicotte. The gamblers are now worried, and Sayles uses a montage of them on the phone beginning with Rothstein to show their response. They arrange to have Lefty Williams (James Read), who will pitch Game Eight, threatened, and, as instructed, he loses the game in the first inning.

It has taken Sayles nearly an hour and a half of screen time to tell the story to this point, leaving him a half hour to show how the scandal was exposed and the trial that resulted. By contrast, Asinof devotes just slightly more than a third of his book to the series and events leading up to it. Clearly, it was Sayles's desire to make a baseball movie, and not "Law and Order, 1920." The result is that, after a montage of Fullerton conducting interviews and newspaper headlines announcing and responding to allegations of a fix, Sayles gives us the story of the grand jury investigation and trial of the eight players in very broad brushstrokes. The key point here is that Rothstein and Comiskey collude in order to protect themselves, while the players, not understanding the legal issues involved, are manipulated by both the prosecution and their own lawyers.

In order to rescue their sport, the owners hire the first commissioner of baseball, Judge Kenesaw Mountain Landis (John Anderson), who is described by Comiskey as "the man who cleaned the reds out of the country during the war." What Sayles doesn't tell us is that Landis imposed very stiff sentences on defendants who were members of the I.W.W. accused of sedition for interfering with the war effort. Landis refused to allow a great deal of potential exculpatory evidence that the Wobblies were interested in economic justice, not in the war itself. Many of the convictions were overturned on appeal. Sayles has him demand, at what is in effect his job interview, absolute power and lifetime tenure, which the owners grant without a murmur of opposition. Anderson looks something like Landis, but even more like Andrew Jackson (he played him on at least one occasion) as he appears on the $20 bill. We suspect immediately that he will be tyrannical and biased against the players.

The trial, as Sayles renders it, is something of a farce. Confessions signed by Cicotte, Jackson, and Williams are missing and cannot be used as evidence. Comiskey appears as a witness for the prosecution, but he is extremely reticent to say anything against the players. Kid Gleason says that they are the greatest team ever to play the game. So, it is not entirely surprising that the players are found innocent, despite the fact that we know most of them are guilty. But what seems to be a moment of triumph for everyone but the prosecution quickly becomes a sad defeat for the players, as Landis is shown announcing that they all will be banned from baseball despite their acquittal. In the end, only the players are punished, the gamblers getting off without a slap on the wrist. The owners suffer nothing for their attempt to cover up the fix, though it is true that Comiskey is now denied most of the players from what had been called the greatest team ever.

Sayles appends a coda to the story, set in New Jersey in 1925, where we see Shoeless Joe (D. B. Sweeney) playing under an assumed name for a semipro team in Hoboken, while some fans speculate about who this mystery player really is. Buck Weaver is in the stands, and he tells the fans that he had seen Joe play and that he was the best. Jackson plays like himself, but Weaver protects his identity, saying, "those guys are all gone now." Weaver had objected to being tried with the others, but his motion for a separate trial was denied. Jackson is usually regarded as the great victim of the scandal, on the grounds that, despite his having confessed to taking money, he actually had a very good series. His ignorance, which is played up throughout the movie, made him an easy target of the other players and the prosecutors. Moreover, since many people believed that, in this era before Babe Ruth and the rabbit ball, Jackson was the greatest player in history, his loss to the game is likewise the saddest. Sayles concludes the film with a freeze-frame of Jackson tipping his hat to the New Jersey crowd, while titles tell us that the eight never played major league ball again and that Buck Weaver tried every year to clear his name. For Sayles, clearly it is Weaver who has been the most unjustly treated.

The commentary in the stands as Jackson plays incognito sums up the lack of a definitive judgment of the players on the filmmaker's part. Weaver calls Jackson "the best," but when a kid asks another fan who Jackson is, he is told, "He's one of them bums from Chicago." The viewer is left to make up his or her own mind about which of these opinions is correct. That is possible because of the film's refusal to offer the viewer an easy, consistent point of identification. While the coda gives the viewer a focus on individuals the rest of the film denied them, its pathos is muted by our lack of identification. On the whole, *Eight Men Out* bears some resemblance to Sergei Eisenstein's films such as *Battleship Potemkin* (1925), where the principal antagonists are not individuals, but classes. Although, unlike *Potemkin*, Sayles's film has many individuals, ultimately, it is the story of workers (the ballplayers) being victimized by two sorts of capitalists, the owners and the gamblers, who in the end team up to protect themselves. But because the workers in this case are complicit in their own downfall, *Eight Men Out* is not a vision of the heroic proletariat, but once again of the impersonal and implacable power with which they ultimately cannot contend. Whereas

Matewan ended on a mixed note of briefly successful resistance coupled with individual tragedy and long-term failure, this film ends without any sense of hope.

Eight Men Out was well received by the critics, and the film was more widely reviewed than most of Sayles's previous efforts. The critics who liked the film praised the baseball scenes, the refusal to oversimplify the complexity of the events, and the acting. The acting is excellent almost across the board, with Cusack and Strathairn standouts as Weaver and Cicotte. Perhaps the weakest performance is Sayles's own as Ring Lardner. His sardonic interventions are meant to be humorous, but often fall flat, perhaps because Sayles plays the writer stiffly, as if the suit and high shirt collar were inhibiting his movement. Those who dissented complained about the film being difficult to follow. One reason for this may be the unsuccessful use of Fullerton and Lardner to provide commentary on the events. They appear regularly throughout the film, but only Fullerton's role in uncovering the scandal is necessary. After a while, we begin to wonder why they are there. Just one reviewer, Rita Kempley of the *Washington Post*, complained about Sayles's "liberal" politics. The film earned about $5.7 million, Sayles's highest gross to date, but not enough to cover its $6 million cost. Distribution problems again may have limited the audience. Sayles blamed Orion Pictures for having bigger fish to fry and complained that independent theaters, where his previous films were typically shown, were being bought up or forced out of business by the expansion of chain multiplexes.

Place and Melodrama: *City of Hope* and *Passion Fish*

Sayles's interest in the evocation of place became clear in *Matewan*, if it wasn't already. But the films he would make next are more focused on place, in part because they have a contemporary setting. *City of Hope* is about New Jersey as much as it is about urban politics and corruption; *Passion Fish* is a story that could not be told in the same way had it been set anywhere other than the bayou country of Louisiana. Sayles will continue to immerse his audiences in specific localities in his films that follow these, but these two films stand out from those before or since by their relationship to melodrama. *City of Hope* is Sayles's most melodramatic film, though the melodrama is largely restricted to one of its multiple plotlines. *Passion Fish* is as much about melodrama as it is one, for here Sayles is explicitly bending Hollywood's most traditionally melodramatic genre, the women's picture. Although we are in the habit of assuming that melodrama and realism have little to do with each other, Peter Brooks has argued that they historically have gone together, for example, describing Balzac's novels as "social melodrama" (181). Sayles makes the connection by reference to playwright Arthur Miller, whose realist family dramas like *Death of a Salesman* he correctly identifies as melodramatic (Crowdus and Quart in Carson, *Interviews* 149).

It would be more than three years, until November of 1991, when Sayles would see the release of his next feature, *City of Hope*. In the meantime, he created and wrote a short-lived TV series, *Shannon's Deal* and published his third novel, *Los Gusanos*. Sayles wanted to take a break from directing, so the layoff was self-imposed. The financing for the new film came relatively easily, with the bulk of it coming from Tristar Home Video. Sayles had long had the idea for the film in mind, but wrote the screenplay very quickly sometime after completing *Eight Men Out*.

City of Hope contradicts two oft-repeated criticisms of Sayles: that he is visually uninteresting and that his films have obvious political messages. Although I've been arguing that that latter is a misreading of any of Sayles's movies, it is patently not the case with this one. Indeed, it could be argued that one of the weaknesses of *City of Hope* is that its politics are not clear enough. Visually, however, the film is quite distinctive, bearing little resemblance to standard Hollywood fare or even to Sayles's previous work. The basic technique is the one Sayles used in the hotel corridor scene in *Eight Men Out*, in which transitions between characters are achieved through "trading," as they move through a continuous take. A trade occurs when the shot shifts from one character to another within a single take, such that our attention is directed to another plotline or story thread. This method achieved two ends. First, it enabled Sayles to shoot a complicated script in a short period of time, allowing him to stay within his $3 million budget. By filming most scenes as mastershots, the director could work much faster than if he had to set up for many shorter takes. Second, he could illustrate visually the connections between seemingly unrelated stories.

Sayles had said that he learned how to make *Return of the Secaucus Seven* visually appealing from watching *Nashville*, which moved between subplots on cuts. In other respects, *Secaucus Seven*, is not much like Altman's film, being a story centered in one space about a group of people all of whom have direct connections to each other. *City of Hope* is much more like *Nashville* in that it is about a large group characters many of whom are not known to each other. And, like *Nashville,* this film is about the city as a single place having a diversity of spaces. But instead of using cuts to motivate subplots, Sayles uses "trades," a technique used only occasionally by Altman. The effect of Altman's cuts is to give us the city as collage, where things happen randomly sometimes because people do accidentally find themselves in the same space. Thus the assassin kills the country singer and not the presidential candidate. The effect of Sayles's trades is to give us the city as a web of sometimes open, sometimes occult connections.

What both films share is the lack of a single story line that unites the whole picture. *City of Hope,* however, does have two stories that run through most of the film. One is story of Nick Rinaldi (Vincent Spano), a close-up of whose face is the opening shot. Nick is the ne'er-do-well son of Joe Rinaldi (Tony Lo Bianco), a building contractor. The first thing Nick does is quit the job his father has arranged for him at a construction site, even though the job doesn't require him to do any work. This act of rebellion characterizes Nick's stance throughout the story. The other main plot involves the political career of Wynn (Joe Morton), a recently elected city councilman. Wynn was previously a professor, and he comes to politics with the idealism of an outsider. But he is an outsider not merely because he is a political neophyte, but because he is both African American and a professor. As the only black on the council, he is outside the majority, but as a middle-class professional, he is an outsider to the African American community he represents. The characters' trajectories go in opposite directions, as Wynn learns how to compromise in order to win the support of his community, while Nick cannot escape himself or the family history that seems to oppress him.

There are about fifty other characters, however, and many subplots that are often but tangentially related to these two longer story lines. The subplot that ties stories of Nick and Wynn together is a plan to tear down an old apartment building in Wynn's district to make way for a new condominium and shopping complex. Joe Rinaldi owns the building, and his firm would build the new one. The problem is that the tenants in the current building don't want to leave despite Joe's refusal of services and failure to maintain it. The investors don't want to wait for the slow process of evicting the tenants, but Joe is unwilling to do anything more until Nick is charged in connection with an attempted robbery at an electronics store. In return for getting the charges dropped, Joe agrees to have a fire set in a supposedly empty wing in order to render the rest of the building uninhabitable. The plan works, except that there are squatters living in the wing where the fire is set, and a baby is killed. The loss of the housing units, occupied mainly by poor African Americans gives Wynn an issue around which to rally his constituents. Joe's complicity in arson and murder shows us the world from which Nick wants desperately to escape, but which has also made him who he is. He is horrified by his father's behavior, and outraged to learn that Joe went along with the crime in order to help him.

Sayles has cited both *Do the Right Thing* (Spike Lee, 1989) and the television series *Hill Street Blues* (Steven Bochco, Michael Kozoll, 1981–87) as influences on *City of Hope* (Smith 182–83). But Sayles correctly identifies Lee's focus as on the microcosm of a single block, whereas his own film is concerned with connections that run throughout a city. *Hill Street Blues* was a groundbreaking treatment of a city police force, but it ultimately had little to do either with the larger community or its politics. Many of the subplots of *City of Hope* concern criminals and cops, but the film also deals with the politics and problems of a midsize American city. It thus resembles much more than either of these predecessors, the more recent television series, *The Wire* (David Simon, 2002–8), with which it shares several cast members. In particular, Sayles's film resembles season two of *The Wire,* which involved a white ethnic community connected to the docks and the African American drug gangs that are a focus of each season. Although *The Wire* is much more a police drama, like *City of Hope* it is a political-realist treatment of the essentially intractable problems of a city. Both keep tangentially related multiple plots in motion, and they move between the personal lives of characters and the institutions that govern them. But where *The Wire* had five seasons, a total of sixty episodes of one hour each, *City of Hope* runs just 130 minutes. The comparison suggests that the kind of picture Sayles wanted to draw is too big for a feature film. While *The*

Wire makes one feel that it has captured the whole, *City of Hope* seems more like a series of anecdotes.

Bould's claim that Sayles is a "naturalist" is perhaps most plausible of *City of Hope*, and one can see the influence of latter-day naturalist writer Nelson Algren. In Algren, the naturalism of Norris and Dreiser gets transmuted by the hard-boiled language and attitude of Cain, Hammett, and the *Black Mask* writers. *The Wire* is the twenty-first-century version of that combination. Most of its characters are as doomed as Norris's McTeague or Frankie Machine from Algren's *The Man with the Golden Arm*. The dedication and gallows humor of some of the cops leavens the story a bit, but the attitude of the series seems to be the same as their professional detachment from the horrors they must investigate.

By comparison, *City of Hope* is a much more emotionally charged representation, more melodramatic than hard-boiled. This sentimentality is both a weakness and a strength. The weakness is most obvious in the treatment of Nick, whose life seems to be a soap opera. After quitting his job, he borrows $50 from his sister, Laurie (Gina Gershon) because he owes a $2000 gambling debt. Apparently in order to make up the difference, he goes along with his friends' scheme to burgle the electronics store. While they get caught in the act, he gets away and finds Angela (Barbara Williams) who he had just met earlier that evening at a bar. It seems to be love at first sight for him, as he insists on walking her home and telling her how special she is. Later they will become lovers, but her ex-husband, Rizzo (Anthony John Denison) remains jealous of anyone who shows her attention. Rizzo is a cop, who warns Nick to stay away from her and will later use the excuse of the robbery warrant to take shot at him. Nick seems to overreact to every situation in which he finds himself, and that emotionality colors the relatively large part of the movie in which he appears. It is perhaps meant to be a study of someone out of control, but given Nick's prominence in the film, we are also invited to feel his pain. The film doesn't convince us, however, that Nick deserves our empathy. The film's final scene, with Joe finding the wounded Nick at the empty construction sight is overwrought from the start, and it ends with Joe screaming for help to the street below, where only the mentally ill Asteroid (David Strathairn) is there to hear.

All he can do is to repeat Joe's cries back to him, just as earlier we had seem him repeating a TV commercial he watched in a store window.

If Nick's story line seems emotionally excessive from beginning to end, the treatment of the two black youths, Tito (Edward Jay Townsend Jr.) and Desmond (Jojo Smollett) seems detached and perhaps somewhat naive. The two are seen being harassed by white cops simply for walking on the wrong side of town, but then, seemingly in an act of racial revenge, they viciously attack a white jogger in the park. When they are picked up and charged with the attack, they invent a story about the man being a homosexual who tried to touch them against their will. The movie portrays the African American community as convinced that the boys are being unfairly prosecuted, and Wynn manages to get the victim, Les (Bill Raymond), to drop the charges by asserting that he will suffer if the boys' allegations are made publicly in a trial. Serious crime in Hudson City is the province of white hoodlums, such as Carl (John Sayles, in one of his best performances), the "brains" behind both the failed burglary and the arson. Yet as *City of Hope* was released, American cities had been experiencing a new wave of gang violence that was related to the spread of crack cocaine in the mid-1980s. John Singleton's *Boyz in the Hood* was released just few months before Sayles's film, and it depicted a much grimmer and more violent world for black kids. Where *Boyz* and *The Wire* chiefly focus on the violence of African American drug gangs, *City of Hope* ignores this problem entirely.

Why it does this is probably the result of Sayles's politics. African American men still tend to show up in mainstream entertainment mainly as criminals, and Sayles here, as in *Brother from Another Planet,* wants to show us the reality that most African Americans are decent, law-abiding citizens. In *City of Hope,* we are reminded that gangs are as American as apple pie, and that earlier generations of immigrants formed ones that grew up to become what we now call "organized crime." By including the crime by Tito and Desmond, Sayles acknowledges the problem, but by connecting it to police harassment, he also offers racism as an explanation. The strength of Sayles's emotional stance toward his story is that it shows he has a politics. *The Wire* is about politics, but it is not clear that it has any of its own. Missing from its picture of Baltimore is any genuine organized resistance. Sayles includes such resistance when he has Wynn lead a march to a fund-raising dinner for the mayor to confront him about condominium project and the lack of housing for the low-income people. This is one of the few hopeful moments in *City of Hope*—another occurs when Desmond seeks out Les and apologizes to him—but its not clear what Wynn thinks the march can accomplish. As we saw with *Matewan*, standing up in the face of oppression is a good in itself, but it is a limited good. Wynn's gesture seems more likely to cement support for him than to change anything in Hudson City.

Once again, Sayles's politics form the background for *City of Hope*, but here they are even less evident than usual in the foreground. The main lesson of the film is not about racism or oppression, but the necessity for compromise. Wynn has to get Tito and Desmond off to show his loyalty to his community even though he believes that boys are lying. Joe is willing to consent to torching the apartment in order to save his son from jail. Sayles clearly doesn't think these compromises are morally equivalent, but in each case someone commits a wrong in order to achieve what he sees as a right. The film suggests that progress may be possible, but only slowly and through compromise. This is not the usual message of the Left, which has traditionally imagined change in the form of revolution or a less violent but still sweeping radical transformation. *City of Hope* is the clearest illustration of this side of Sayles's political realism.

Counseling compromise is not usually very exciting, and when the counsel comes in the form of a complex, visually innovative and narratively fragmented film, it is unlikely to attract a mass audience. *City of Hope* grossed only about $1.2 million, attracting what certainly was Sayles's smallest audience to date. The film was fairly widely reviewed, but the notices were greatly divided. It got strongly positive reviews from such prominent critics as Roger Ebert in *Chicago Sun-Times* and Vincent Canby in the *New York Times*, who called it Sayles's "most invigorating achievement to date." Richard Corliss in *Time* called it "a stately mess" ("Dead End"), and the *Washington Post*'s Kempley, predictably, found it "visually dull and topically abstract." Sayles by this point seems to have developed supporters and opponents among the critical establishment, and the reviews of this film seemed to follow accordingly.

Sayles's first three pictures dealt with women centrally. In *Secaucus Seven*, the women are given equal visibility, and they are more economically successful than the men. *Lianna* focuses on the lesbian community, and *Baby It's You* is much more Jill's film than it is the Sheik's. After that movie, however, Sayles's films became more male-centered, and criticism of women's lack of prominence began to be heard. Maggie Renzi had also felt that Sayles had been neglecting women, and she urged Sayles to next make "the hospital one," the film that would become *Passion Fish.* The film was financed by home-video presales, and a distribution deal was reached with Miramax, the independent company that had changed the industry with its promotion and distribution of *sex, lies, and videotape* in 1989.

Renzi wanted Sayles to make a story for women, and what Sayles came up with is a bent version of the old Hollywood genre, the women's picture. These films, typified by such titles as *Now, Voyager* (Irving Rapper, 1942), *Letter from an Unknown Woman* (Max Ophüls, 1948), and many of Douglas Sirk's melodramas from the 1950s, are about women not getting what they want. According to Mary Ann Doane, they are not even about desire in the primary sense, but rather "the desire to desire." The women's picture almost always ends with the woman's resignation to the failure of her romantic dreams, a failure that is not her fault. As Doane observes, "the woman almost always gives up everything . . . for the sake of love" (109). *Passion Fish* is not about the failure of romantic love, but it is about a woman who loses almost everything, and who is redeemed by a difficult relationship with a woman she hires to be her nurse.

Passion Fish represents the return to the small-scale filmmaking of *Secaucus Seven* and *Lianna*, and it was a significant shift from the much larger scale of his films beginning with *Matewan*. The story for *Passion Fish*, which was one he had been thinking about for some time, Sayles attributes to two sources. He called it "the hospital story" because it drew on his experiences working as an orderly in hospitals and nursing homes during high school and college. The filmic inspiration was Ingmar Bergman's *Persona* (1966), in which a nurse is put in charge of an actress who can't talk and finds that the actress's persona is melding with hers. People, Sayles says, "would go on about the symbolism. I thought it was about a nurse and a patient, and I always reckoned it would be a good idea to do a comedy American version" (Johnson in Carson, *Interviews* 165). *Passion Fish*, however, might be considered a comedy only in comparison to Bergman's intense, psychological drama. While there are moments of comic relief and the ending is not anymore tragic than the beginning, Sayles's film lacks both the laughs and a genuinely happy ending that film audiences expect from comedy.

Passion Fish opens with May-Alice Culhane (Mary McDonnell) waking up in a hospital bed, not fully able to remember what has happened to her. The first thing she does is to stab at the button on the hospital remote, her panic suggesting that she wants to call the nurse. What she does instead is to turn on the TV. Oddly to us and perhaps to her, she sees herself on a soap opera, playing a woman who has amnesia, who says "All I remember is—I wasn't happy, was I?" She's talking to an African American woman, apparently a medical professional of some kind, a pairing that foreshadows what will the be film's major focus, her relationship with a black nurse, Chantelle (Alfre Woodard). This opening in medias res is typical of Sayles, but it is unusual for this kind of story. Hollywood typically would start with the accident that put May-Alice in the hospital. Before the scene ends, she will discover that she can't move her legs, but she will not remember why. On television, a man will tell her it's so nice to see her out of the hospital, and she will tell him she feels fine. It is a painful reminder of the difference between fantasy and reality.

It will be after the credit sequence, where we see May-Alice having difficulty learning how to cope physically and psychologically with her condition, when we learn that she was hit trying to get into a cab to go get her legs waxed. The errand seems almost a pun for what happened, getting her legs *whacked*. But it also makes her accident absurd, especially in the context of the women's picture. Where the genre's typical heroine gives up everything for love, May-Alice seems to have given up almost everything to lose a little hair. May-Alice hasn't lost love, it's true, but she has lost the hope it. Since she can no longer feel the sensations of sex, she is a literal illustration of the desire to desire.

Sayles has said that he chose to make May-Alice a former soap-opera star because "these depths of despair naturally bring the soap opera to mind, and rather than skirt the issue, I chose to attack it head-on" (*Silver City* 322). Sayles sees soap operas as a genre that must be involving without being too upsetting. He argues that soaps require a style of acting that is intentionally shallow in order to buffer the audience from deep emotions. *Passion Fish*, of course, is meant to be the opposite of that, a film that will confront the despair associated with a catastrophic injury. But even though we call them both melodramas, women's pictures are not soap operas. A two-hour film is not under the same obligation to refrain from upsetting the audience. Still, women's pictures have traditionally rewarded viewers willing to suffer with the heroine by offering some measure of redemption in the conclusion. Women's pictures never have conventional Hollywood happy endings, but they are not full-on tragedies either. Their purpose has been to counsel women's acceptance of limitations that they cannot change. As Charlotte Vance (Bette Davis) in *Now, Voyager* puts it to the lover she has given up for the sake of his marriage, " Oh, Jerry, don't let's ask for the moon. We have the stars."

Sayles clearly does not want to urge women's acceptance of patriarchal limitations, but his story nevertheless is about the acceptance of loss. He has said that the film is about the loss that inevitably comes with aging, and he sees *Passion Fish* as dealing with the same issue as *Baby, It's You* and *Secaucus Seven,* the recognition of new limits at different stages of life. "*Passion Fish* is very much about being forty and having hit unpassable ceilings" (Smith 198). Yet this explanation doesn't explain the severity of May-Alice's accidentally imposed limitations. Loss in the women's picture is always excessive; otherwise, how could tears be jerked?

In discussing *City of Hope*, I noted that realism and melodrama are closely related in that both deal with mundane social life. One traditionally assumed difference, however, has been precisely that of the emphasis put on ordinary versus extreme events. Another is the emotional temperature of their presentation. *City of Hope* seemed to slide into melodrama because of the emotional excess associated with Nick and his relationship to his father. *Passion Fish* largely avoids this slide by maintaining a cooler attitude and achieving a certain distance from its characters. Although we begin the film with May-Alice, Sayles limits our identification with her by not giving us any shots from her point of view until after the credit sequence, except of the television, where she is watching herself. As long as she remains in the hospital, we don't see the faces of the people with whom she interacts, making her seem isolated from us as well. The camera seems to be an almost clinical observer. The purpose of this may be to tell us something about the lack of genuine human interaction in a hospital, but it results in the viewer wondering what to feel.

That begins to change only when we see May-Alice in physical therapy with Louise (Maggie Renzi) after she has moved back to Louisiana. Not only is this the first time Sayles uses the shot/reverse shot pattern to present human interaction, but it is also the first time that May-Alice deals with another human as a person and not a thing. It is hard to feel sympathy for someone who seems incapable of recognizing the feelings of others. Unlike most women's pictures, the emotional response to loss we see most often in *Passion Fish* is not sadness, but anger. May-Alice may be clinically depressed, but we are not encouraged to cry for her. While she does interact emotionally with the stream of nurses the agency sends, the interaction is off-putting because her anger, however understandable it is as a response to her incapacity, is misdirected at them.

When Chantelle arrives, about fifteen minutes into the film, Sayles begins to invite us into the story by encouraging us to identify with her. We see her get off a Greyhound bus, and she is first shown in a long shot, making her look small and isolated in landscape that includes an oil or chemical plant in the background. There's a cut to a close-up of her, as she looks warily around at a place we guess is very unfamiliar. The other nurses have simply appeared in May-Alice's house, but Chantelle is introduced to us and introduces herself to her new employer. Although we are encouraged to identify with Chantelle, we are also led to wonder about her, since we are told very little about her background.

May-Alice's rudeness and anger at her previous nurses is to some extent excused by their own flaws. She is equally unpleasant to Chantelle when she first arrives—for example, she can't remember Chantelle's name, even after it is repeated several times—but Chantelle does nothing to make us feel she might merit such abuse. We see that she is trying, which means both wanting to help May-Alice by doing the things her paralysis prevents her from doing, but also to understand and accept her anger. She says that she needs the job, and so she tries not entirely out of an altruistic imperative but also out of self-interest.

One might wonder reading this account of *Passion Fish,* or indeed, having just seen the film, why this story was of interest to someone whose other films seem mainly devoted to issues of politics and power. Part of the answer is that, according to Sayles, *Passion Fish* is also about power, though not power in a sense we usually think of as political. What Sayles learned from his experiences as an orderly is that people who take jobs as private nurses undergo "an incredible loss of power," because they have to do pretty much anything their patient demands. But there is also the way in which the patient is powerless, and utterly dependent on the nurse. This was a strange power relationship "because one person was in power because he was healthy and could walk around and the other person was powerful because he was the one who had economic power and signed the checks" (Smith 194). In America, Sayles notes, there's a racial dimension to this because the nurse is likely to be black and the patient white. That fact opens up a political dimension of the film, highlighted not so much in their relationship, but by their interaction with others. For example, May-Alice's friends from high school, Precious and Ti-Marie, assume Chantelle is a servant, and complain about the difficulty of finding good help.

The power struggle between May-Alice and Chantelle seems at points like it may come to dictate both their behaviors, so the primary goal of each is to one-up the other. But this is not how their relationship turns out. In fact, although they do not become close friends, they do begin to help each other and accept that they need each other. May-Alice learns when Chantelle's ex-husband shows up that she is a recovering drug addict. This fact explains part of her mission to get May-Alice to stop drinking, but it also explains Chantelle's desperate need for the job. It's not just the income she needs but to show that she can live a straight, responsible life. The urgency of that is made clear toward the end of the film, when we learn that Chantelle has a daughter whose custody she lost. Her daughter is being raised by her grandfather, but Chantelle wants her back.

With Chantelle's help, May-Alice finds things to live for, including photography, gardening, and cooking, and she stops drinking herself to death. With May-Alice's help, Chantelle learns that she can take care of someone else, that she can stay off drugs, and that she has the hope of being a mother to her child. Both women have the kinds of relationships they are mentally and physically able to with men. Chantelle does not want a serious relationship and is happy to see Sugar (Vondie Curtis-Hall), a local horse trainer, casually. May-Alice is attracted to Rennie

(David Strathairn), a local handyman whom she knew slightly in high school, and he may be the perfect object of her affection. Though he clearly is attracted to her, he is unlikely to want to marry her. He is married to a deeply religious woman with whom he has many children, but whose extremely restrictive beliefs clearly chafe. Unlike in most women's pictures, however, neither of these men is as important to the women as they are to each other.

Place is extremely important to *Passion Fish*, and the place depicted is one we would not have guessed would interest Sayles. He claims that when on a vacation in Louisiana they stayed at some friends' house on a lake, and he told Maggie, "This is the place where the story about the woman in the wheelchair has to happen." The film is full of music and landscapes that are specific to the region of Jennings and Lake Arthur. Rennie takes both women out on a tour of the bayou, and although neither of them has had much use for nature, they both are fascinated by what they see (see figure 10). It is on this trip that the film's title is

Figure 10. Chantelle (Alfre Woodard), Rennie (David Strathairn), and Mary-Alice (Mary McDonnell) explore the bayou.

explained: it's a Cajun custom to tell fortunes based on the contents of the bellies of fish, and Rennie opens one to find two little fish intact. He calls them "passion fish," and he asks each woman to squeeze one for luck in love. It is significant that in the beginning Chantelle can't get May-Alice to leave the house, but in the film's last scene, she asks to take the boat out to the middle of lake.

May-Alice seems to be making the best of her bad situation, when her former producer, Vance, shows up, urging her to come back to her old role. They will incorporate her accident into the story, and make it more serious by having her character be blind, as well. While this detail and the whole conversation with Vance are clearly a part of Sayles's send-up of the soap opera as a genre, it puts May-Alice off, though why this is so is unclear. Apparently, May-Alice has also learned to despise the job she previously held, even though being asked back to it would seem to offer not just a significant ego boost, but a future less bleak than the one she has been living. Turning the job down means that she and Chantelle can continue to help each other, but is that a motive for refusing Vance's offer? Or, are we supposed to see May-Alice's refusal as evidence of her personal growth, taking seriously her remark that "it's either Friday nights at ten or nothing"? Like most of Sayles's films, this one ends indeterminately. Both women have achieved something, but what their futures will bring, we do not know. This lack of closure is a significant revision of the weepie formula, which wants you to sympathize with its characters and not to think about them.

Passion Fish opened to great reviews that came from virtually everywhere, including critics like Rita Kempley who had nothing nice to say about any of his previous films. This less overtly political film clearly did not provoke the usual knee-jerk response from the right-wingers or the *l'art pour l'art* crowd. The performances of McDonnell and Woodard received near universal acclaim, and both received Golden Globe nominations for best actress and supporting actress, respectively. McDonnell also received an Oscar nomination for Best Actress, and the film earned Sayles his first such nomination for best original screenplay. In 1992 its distributor, Miramax, was riding high on the success of *The Crying Game* (Neil Jordan, 1992), and it aggressively promoted Sayles's film as well. The film opened in December in New York and L.A. to qualify for the Academy Awards for 1992, and it was supposed to close again in late

January. It did well enough, however, that Miramax decided to keep it open until its national release date (Ebert in Carson, *Interviews* 161). In the end, *Passion Fish* registered a decent box-office gross of $5.4 million, about $2 million over costs, which apparently satisfied Miramax, although it did not put Sayles in the company of Steven Soderbergh or Neil Jordan (Biskind 148).

Stories

Sayles's next four films share a concern with storytelling, as Bould has shown (122–58). While it would be a mistake to see this focus as primarily self-reflexive, these films do show us Sayles thinking creatively about the way stories function in our culture. Perhaps because of this new self-consciousness about storytelling, the films in this group also often point away from the immediate here and now to a more mythic, psychoanalytic, or simply universally human level of reality. Despite this, these films remain realist in many or most significant dimensions.

After completing the filming of *Passion Fish*, Sayles began to work on *The Secret of Roan Inish*, a film rooted in the Gaelic legend of the *selkies*, beings who sometimes take the shape of seals and sometimes of humans. Based on Rosalie K. Fry's children's book, *The Secret of Ron Mor Skerry*, the project was one suggested by Maggie Renzi, who had read the book as a child. She had argued that there was a lack of good films for children. But the film Sayles made, while certainly appropriate for children, can't be considered a children's film, especially by the standards of its moment. Sayles has called it a "'family film' in the same way that *Treasure Island* . . . or *To Kill a Mockingbird* are family films" (Chanko in Carson, *Interviews* 181). These are films told from a child's perspective and accessible to children, but that adults can appreciate on a different level. While *Roan Inish* has fantastic elements, it is firmly rooted in place, history, and mundane reality, all of which account for much more of the film than does fantasy. While it is the most atypical film Sayles has made, it nevertheless has much in common with his other work in general, and it especially seems to pave the way for his next film, *Lone Star*.

After having been able to raise money for his last three movies relatively easily, Sayles was again struggling to finance *Roan Inish*. He had to personally put up a third of the film's $5 million budget to get the production started. The remainder of the money was promised by Jones Intercable of Denver, but they kept changing the deal in their favor. The crew had to begin work without knowing whether there would be enough money to finish the film (Molyneaux 210–11). The film eventually came in under budget, but Sayles also had trouble finding a distributor. Shot in the summer of 1993, the film would not see general release until February of 1995. Before that it was presented at both the Toronto and Sundance film festivals, the first film of Sayles to be included in the latter. After the studios' "independent" subsidiaries turned the film down, it was picked up by First Look International, a small company that had done more home video than theatrical distribution.

Roan Inish begins with a seal's eye view of a boat carrying Fiona Coneely (Jeni Courtney) back to Donegal to stay with her grandparents. But since we don't yet see the seal, the film's opening is disorienting. Flashbacks show us Fiona's mother's recent burial, an industrial laundry where her father has found work in Glasgow, and finally the pub where he is drinking instead of working. The pub scene is shot much like the opening of *Passion Fish*, in that we do not see the faces of Fiona's interlocutors, the camera remaining at her eye level and on her face. The barmaid suggests that she would be happier living with the "old people," and we return to the boat. This time there is a shot/reverse shot sequence that shows Fiona and the seal staring at each other, while a seagull seems to be accompanying her in the air overhead. This is the first intimation of what will become clear later—Fiona has a special ability to communicate with these creatures. It is appropriate that we see her in a visual relationship with them before we see her in such a relationship with any human beings.

Fiona arrives at her grandparent's small cottage by walking up a hill from the sea. The whitewashed dwelling is set in lush green grass on which a few cows are grazing. This is one of few scenes, however, that looks like the Ireland of travel brochures. The landscapes of the film are beautiful, but they are also rugged and include rocks, sand, and sea. Haskell Wexler's photography renders their beauty, but it also makes them look natural and, sometimes, threatening. He consistently avoids the gloss of travelogues or any sense that the land itself is enchanted or unreal. This is not a movie set in a dreamscape or fairyland. It is, however, about a world apart from the late twentieth century. The events of the film's primary narrative take place around 1949, less than the sixty years that would by convention make the film "historical." But since this is a story about the persistence of traditional ways of life, it seems more removed from the present than that date would suggest. Because of the remote locations used, Sayles did not have to go to great lengths to re-create the period.

One of clearest examples of the film's antimodernism is the role that storytelling plays in it. Sayles has said that one of the reasons the film is set in this timeframe is so that Fiona can imagine "the events we see through her eyes in a way that is untouched by film or television. When her grandfather tells her these stories, she sees them literally . . . without special effects" (Black in Carson, *Interviews* 173). Fiona's grandfather, Hugh (Mick Lally), tells her stories about the island, Roan Inish, where the family used to live and which they can see from the grandparents' cottage. The first of these stories is about his great-grandfather, Sean Michael (Fergal McElherron), who was thrown out of school for insisting on speaking Irish during a time when "the English were still a force in the country." He is shown attacking his English schoolmaster with his fists and cursing at him in Irish. Fiona's grandmother, Tess (Eileen Colgan), objects to the use of such language around a child, but Fiona doesn't understand. She has not learned Irish, a condition symbolic of what Ireland has lost as a result of colonization. Sean Michael is symbolic not only of Irish resistance—the story will end with him dying at fifty in jail for running arms to Irish rebels—but of the Coneelys' deep connection to the sea for he survives a storm that killed his father, brothers, and other male relatives. Washed up on the beach, Sean Michael is found by women who revive him by lying him between two cows that lend him their body heat, an instance of the family's bond with the animal world. That bond is revealed to be even stronger when Sean Michael tells the women who found him that "it was a seal that brought me here."

The story is told mainly in Hugh's voice-over with the sepia-toned images of the events as Fiona sees them in her mind's eye. The pacing is deliberate, with periods in which the voice-over is replaced by music. Sayles's detractors often complain about the slowness of his films, but here he is clearly choosing a pace that is consistent with the traditional culture the film is depicting. Children raised on video games or the frenetic pace of contemporary children's television or movies were likely to have found this film an unfamiliar experience. Sayles was unwilling to pander to this audience's expectations for fancy special effects either, as the only gadgetry used in the film were several animatronic seals. Instead of wowing us with technological magic or cliffhanging suspense, the director asks us to identify with Fiona, to share not only her point of view, but also her hopes and beliefs.

The next story Hugh tells Fiona is of the day the family left Roan Inish, and her infant brother Jamie was lost when his cradle was swept out to sea. Fiona can't understand why no one has mentioned Jamie, and she accuses her grandfather of wanting her to forget him. Hugh introduces the story by saying it was a strange day, like a bad dream from which one cannot awake. The story itself is presented without voice-over and without dialogue except for cries of the baby's name when his family realizes his boat-shaped cradle has floated off of the beach. The day is sunny and bright, but its strangeness is confirmed by the behavior of the gulls, which angrily attack the men who are moving their possessions from the island's cottages in a scene reminiscent of Hitchcock's *The Birds* (1963). While no one is seriously injured, the birds seem to have been creating diversion so that the movement of Jamie's cradle would not be noticed. After the men give chase, the weather turns stormy and they cannot reach the cradle, which drifts farther from them despite their hard rowing. Back in the present, Hugh concludes the story by saying "I don't know how the cradle could have made up so much speed. The sea had taken him, poor, wee Jamie. It was angry with us for leaving Roan Inish." Compared to the way Sean Michael's story was presented, the presentation of this story makes it seem more real, despite its strange content. That may be because Fiona, though she says she could not remember that day, was there when it happened. This is a story about the most important event in her young life, and it leaves open the hope, to which Fiona gives voice, that Jamie might somehow still be alive.

The final story is told not by Hugh, but by Fiona's father's cousin, Tadhg, about how Liam, the first Coneely on Roan Inish, married a selkie long ago when only Irish was spoken there. Fiona meets Tadhg cleaning fish in town, and she is warned that he is slightly crazy, as the temper he shows to his coworkers illustrates. Most members of the family have light eyes and hair, but Tadhg, like Jamie, has black hair and dark eyes. He explains that these anomalous offspring, who seem to take preternaturally to the sea, get their characteristics from the selkie. The story is told in voice-over, without dialogue. We see Liam (Gerard Rooney) discover the selkie (Susan Lynch) as she transforms from seal into woman. Sayles stages the event as a simple matter of the selkie shedding its sealskin to reveal human flesh. Liam finds the sealskin, putting the selkie within his power, and he brings her back to Roan Inish to be his wife. When she becomes pregnant, she instructs Liam to make a cradle like a boat, the origin of the one in which Jamie was lost (see figure 11). After bearing many children, the selkie discovered where Liam had hidden her skin, and she returned to the sea. After that, we are told, it was forbidden to harm a seal on the island. Tadhg concludes his story by saying, "welcome back, Fiona Coneely. We've been waiting." Though Tadhg's craziness may cause us to doubt his story, it seems to explain many of the things we had previously witnessed, and it turns Fiona into something more than just a little girl mourning her lost brother.

In the meantime, Fiona has gotten Hugh to take her to Roan Inish, where she sees that someone has been living in her old house and notices small footprints in the sand. After she hears Tadhg's story, her cousin,

Figure 11. The selkie (Susan Lynch) and the cradle.

Eamon (Richard Sheridan) takes her back to island. She falls asleep in a cottage and dreams of the selkie. When she awakes she walks to the other side of the island, sees her seal friend, whom she calls Jax, sunning himself on the rocks, and then spies Jamie romping in a green field. He runs away from her, gets into his cradle, and floats away. When she returns to the mainland, she learns that her grandparents will have to leave their house because the landlord wants to rent it for the summer to foreign tourists. This gives the old folks a need to return to island. The next day is foggy, and Fiona is told she can't go out on the sea with her grandfather and cousin. She climbs into a tethered dinghy to get a better look at Jax, but the boat mysteriously slips out into the sea with the seal at its side. It drifts through the fog and ends up at Roan Inish. She finds Jamie this time sharing a meal with a seal in a cottage, and while he runs away from her again, this cements her and our confidence that her brother really is alive.

Fiona and Eamon decide that they might be able to persuade their grandparents to move back to the island if they rebuild the cottages. In a montage sequence, Sayles shows us the kids cleaning, painting, and rethatching the dwellings. Labor is part of every Sayles film, but this is about as unalienated as labor can be. Both children have decided that they belong on the island, and they are willing to work hard to achieve that goal. After fixing up the cottages, Fiona lets it slip to her grandmother that she has seen Jamie. The grandmother insists that they go to the island, and when they arrive they do find Jamie, whom the seals seem to urge to return to his family. The family is reunited, not just with its lost child, but also with its members who live in the sea and with the land where it belongs.

Sayles is working here at the level of wish and myth that has been largely absent in his earlier work. The sense that humans and animals are deeply connected is one that runs through the mythology of many different peoples, and the wish to be able to talk with animals is apparently very old and very common. While Sayles sees the idea of the selkie as having come out of guilt about killing these anthropomorphic-looking creatures, the story in the context of the 1990s raises larger issues about humans' relationship to nature. The antimodernism of this story is of a piece with much environmentalism, with the back-to-the-land ethic that Joni Mitchell named in "Woodstock" as an imperative to get "back to the garden." This perspective is often identified with the left, but it has not traditionally been so. Karl Marx famously complained about "the idiocy of rural life," and peasants were always understood to be conservative because they were fearful of change. Sayles clearly sees virtue not only in the Coneelys' sense of kinship with nature, but also in the simple, largely pre–consumer society that goes along with it. The independence of these people from the larger industrial world around them reminds one of his own independence from the film industry. In each case, independence is not a matter of individualism, but of embeddedness in a community.

Much of the power of *Roan Inish* derives from its strong evocation of place, which this film takes to a new level. For example, by using Irish actors, Sayles is able to give us the language of this place, of an English not spoken by Americans or the English. Mason Daring's music, which always contributes to the sense of place in Sayles's films, is here especially successful. This may be in part because Irish music is familiar to Americans because it lies at root of much of our own folk and country traditions. Daring's music sounds authentic, yet it does not sound so familiarly Irish as to be a cliché. The rugged Donegal coast is visually distinctive, and Wexler's use of natural light makes it look sometimes tranquil and others brooding. By the end of the film we feel this story could not have been told about any other place.

That brings us to the second wish that *Roan Inish* expresses, for a deep connection to place, that is, for a home. The psychological, rather than social or political, truth of this story is that we all as adults are in some way or another lost, and we wish to return to a home that ceased to exist when we grew up. Children fear such loss, which they may dimly sense is in their future, and they find stories of return reassuring. We will see something of the same psychoanalytic logic in the mythic resonances of *Lone Star.* The idea of belonging to a particular place may be especially attractive to Americans who often feel rootless. We envy those who know where they belong, even if they are exiled from that place. Sayles has said that one of the reasons he moved the setting of the film from the Scotland of the book to Ireland was the sense that it is "obsessed with loss—their national sovereignty, their language, their sons and daughters, and a certain past, [which] seemed perfect for this particular story, which is about the loss of an island and a way of life"

(Smith 208). But the story is about restoration of what is lost. It is about losing and finding one's place, and, as Sayles has said, losing and finding "identity" (Black in Carson, *Interviews* 173). Identity will be a major concern of *Lone Star*, but it is treated quite differently in the two films. In *Roan Inish*, identity is defined by place, family, and nationality, and it becomes problematic only when these are abandoned or lost. One could argue, however, that that is a nostalgic conception of identity; for most Americans, as *Lone Star* explores, identity is much more complicated.

The Secret of Roan Inish was well received by critics and earned Sayles his largest gross yet, about $6 million. First Look was willing to give the film time to develop word of mouth, and the film enjoyed long runs at art houses in places like Portland, Oregon, and Minneapolis. Critics found much to like and little to criticize about the project, and they often urged adults to go see it.

Lone Star

Sayles had wanted to make *Men with Guns* next, but his lack of personal funds meant that project would need to be postponed. After the difficulties of financing and distributing *The Secret of Roan Inish*, Sayles spent some time writing screenplays for hire and doctoring scripts. One of those projects was a screenplay for Rob Reiner on the 1960s. While the film was never produced, the connection to Reiner resulted in an invitation from Castle Rock Entertainment to submit a proposal for a film that Sayles would direct. He decided to propose *Lone Star*, and the proposal was quickly accepted, with a budget of $5 million. Sayles has said he had never financed a film so easily.

If *Matewan* and *Eight Men Out* are historical films, *Lone Star* is a film about history, both public and personal. It is also a film about cultural and personal identity. Like *Matewan*, it is a film that owes a great deal to a familiar Hollywood genre, in this case the murder mystery. But unlike the earlier film, *Lone Star* does not treat the detective as a mythic figure; rather, this is a film about demythologizing the past. But if it is critical of dominant cultural mythology, it nevertheless taps into unconscious patterns in a way that is more reminiscent of the novels of William Faulkner than it is of other films. Although *Lone Star*, which, as the title implies, is set in Texas also displays some of the familiar markers of the Western, such as six-guns and ten-gallon hats, its plot and themes fall outside of that genre's conventions. The Western is properly considered part of the characters' background, because some of them seem to behave as if they were living in that world. Charlie Wade and Buddy Deeds are legends, and thus have something in common with Doc Holiday and Wyatt Earp.

Lone Star is also a film that shows no evidence of its low budget. Shot in super 35 mm format by Stuart Dryburgh, who had previously been director of photography on Jane Campion's *The Piano* (1993), *Lone Star* looks stunning. It has all the visual gloss of a big-budget movie, a look that in part may have benefited from the natural light of the location. In any case, *Lone Star* lacks the slightly faded or cloudy-day look that Sayles consciously went for in much of both *Matewan* and *Eight Men Out*. The film's gloss does not distract us from its realism because the production design remains true to Sayles's sense of the ordinary. Moreover, the film's style is striking because of the way camera movement and lighting are used in the service of the film's narrative and its themes.

Like many of Sayles's films, *Lone Star* tells multiple stories. The film represents three different ethnic communities in the fictional border town of Frontera: Anglos, who have ruled the community since the Mexican War; Mexicans, who have lived there since before that war, are the largest in number, and are in the process of claiming political power; and African Americans, the smallest group, many of whom are associated with a nearby army base and are thus not permanent residents. Each community is represented by a family of multiple generations in which the relationship of an adult to his or her parent of the same gender is central to the story. By the end, we will learn of a history that connects all three communities, but the narrative threads of *Lone Star* remain distinctive, just as the three communities will continue to be distinct from one another.

Lone Star opens with a slow panning shot of a desert landscape. In the foreground it finds Cliff (Steven Mandillo) with a botanical field guide, identifying plants. In the background, we can make out Mikey (Stephen J. Lang), who tells Cliff to come look at something he's found. It turns out to be a human skull, and there's a Masonic ring with it. After Sheriff Sam Deeds (Chris Cooper) arrives, a rust-encrusted sheriff's badge is discovered. There is a cut to Pilar (Elizabeth Peña), a teacher discussing one of her students with his mother, an African American, reassuring her that he is not involved with gangs. While in *City of Hope*, Sayles used in-shot "trades" to connect disparate plots, here the different narrative threads are marked by abrupt edits. Pilar learns from another teacher that her son, Amado (Gonzallo Castillo), is missing from school, and there's a cut to a deputy picking him up after catching him trying to install a stolen CD player in a pickup truck. It's the Mexican American teacher's kid who is in trouble.

Two contemporary stories having been set in motion, the scene shifts to the Café Santa Barbara, where three older men are sitting, telling stories about the former Sheriff, Buddy Deeds. One is Hollis (Clifton James), formerly deputy under Buddy and currently the town's mayor. Another is Fenton (Tony Frank), who calls the current Sheriff, who is Buddy's son, "all hat and no cattle" just before Sam walks up to the table. They begin a conversation about the upcoming ceremony to name the courthouse after Buddy, and Fenton complains that there had been opposition to the plan from Mexican Americans. Fenton represents the uncensored voice of Anglo resentment in losing privilege. We are also seeing in the background, Mercedes Cruz (Miriam Colon), owner of the café and a city council woman, and we are told she voted for Buddy. She seems to know but does not acknowledge that Sam is looking at her.

Fenton asks Hollis to tell the story of how Buddy became sheriff, but he protests that it had been told a million times. Sam says, "I'd like to hear it. Your version of it." There is a series of shots of the three characters, but as Hollis gets into his story, camera tracks slowly closer to him, and then pans down toward the table to show first his arms and hands and then a close-up of a basket of tortillas. The historical shift is made then, as we see another hand, with a ring prominently displayed, lift up some tortillas, to find money hidden under them (see figure 12). The camera then pans up to show Charlie Wade (Kris Kristofferson) talking about the payoff, which is to insure that Charlie will not make trouble about the "wetbacks" who work in the café's kitchen. The camera then pans left to show Buddy Deeds (Matthew McConaughey). After he asks a question, the shot ends with a cut back to Charlie, and the camera pulls back to show a third person at the table, a young Hollis (Jeff Monahan). One shot has thus tied together present and past and linked Buddy and Charlie, who in the next few shots will be defined

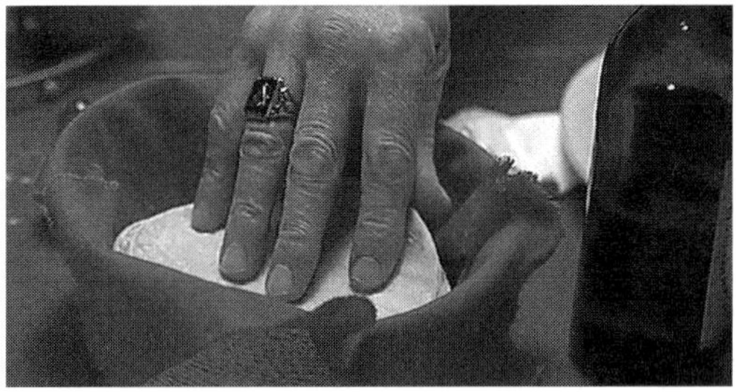

Figure 12. A basket of tortillas as historical bridge and money drop for Charlie Wade.

as antagonists. The shot embodies the idea that the past remains alive, and that people past and present are inextricably bound to one another. This technique will be used throughout the film to move between past and present.

This seamless temporal shift is accomplished not only by the long take, but also by lighting. When we first entered the café, it was broad daylight. But when the camera pans up to show Charlie, it has become night. The café itself, which looks clean and well kept in the present, looks dark and dingy in the past. But it is significant that the story Hollis is telling took place where he is telling it. History in *Lone Star* is there, present in the form of people and things that were part of it. Only the Alamo, the film's synecdoche for the larger history of Texas, is missing, and that too is, as we will see, is a meaningful absence.

Charlie and Buddy get into an argument over the payoff, which the latter refuses to have anything to do with. He threatens Charlie, suggesting that he leave town before he winds up dead or in jail. The two appear ready to draw on one another, but Charlie fires Buddy and says "you're a dead man" before he and Hollis walk out of the café. We return to the present when the camera pans away from Buddy ordering another beer to Sam standing in behind him to the right while Hollis repeats the last words Buddy has said. Then Fenton picks up the story, initiating another pattern that will be repeated throughout *Lone Star*: stories begun by one teller being completed by another. In this case, however, Hollis comes back in to report that "We made our pick up at Roderick's place, and nobody's seen hide nor hair of him since." Before the conversation ends, both Fenton and Sam agree that there will never be another one like Buddy, and Hollis calls him "my salvation."

There's a cut to a group of soldiers in fatigues standing in formation and being addressed by Del (Joe Morton), a colonel and base commanding officer, who is affirming that he runs a tight ship. This represents the third narrative strand, which will involve both Del's father, Otis (Ron Canada), and his son, Chet (Eddie Robinson). Otis owns Big O's, a roadhouse that is the main entertainment spot for African Americans, including those from the base. Soon we see Chet peering into Big O's, and he finally surreptitiously enters the club. We see him holding an ad for the place and looking at Otis as if to determine whether he's in the right place. A man is shot, and Otis finds Chet and tells him he wasn't there and to slip out the back. The two apparently know who each is, but they don't know each other. We will learn that Del has not had any contact with Otis for years, so the boy had never met his grandfather. The theme of conflict between fathers and sons thus echoes between Sam's story and Del's.

This theme has led many academic critics to discuss the film in Oedipal terms. Indeed, most academics at least mention what they see as Oedipal relations between fathers and sons. Susan Felleman reads *Lone Star* as yet another Oedipal film in a long line, and, following Harold Bloom's theory of the anxiety of influence, she treats its relationship to it predecessors as itself Oedipal. Felleman's essay is a reminder of 1970s film theory, which treated the Oedipus complex as fundamental to Hollywood cinema and an indication of its phallocentrism. Bould points out the limitations of this theory and the readings it fosters, arguing that "In its crudest applications, and many of its commonest ones, the Oedipal complex strips texts of their particularity and diversity, flensing them of detail so that they conform to the structure of myth, a unificatory tendency completely at odds with *Lone Star*'s politics" (134). But not all those who discuss the film in these terms are guilty of this reduction. Rebecca Gordon refers at length to one of the major Lacanian film theorists, Kaja Silverman, to show that *Lone Star* does not simply repeat the old story (220). George Handley notes that "rather than choosing to literally blind themselves, as does Oedipus, once Sam and Pilar discover their dark secret, they exercise their agency to assign new meaning to their 'blood'" (175). Geoffrey Bakewell discusses *Lone Star* in relation to

Oedipus Rex rather than to Freud, but he concludes something similar, that "it puts forward a serious claim that one of our most enduring social taboos is in fact more a cultural construct than a stable moral value." He suggests that "Forget Oedipus" would be an apt title for the film (48).

My own view, however, is that we should forget Oedipus because its connection to *Lone Star* is tangential. The versions of Oedipus involved in most readings derive from Lacan, and they tend to ignore Freud's primary use of the myth in the context of child development within a two-parent family. *Oedipal* is used by most critics simply to mean a conflict between fathers and sons—or as in Handley, any conflict between dominant and subordinate—rather than conflict resulting from jealousy over possession of the mother. What is striking about *Lone Star* is that none of the families of the adult sons include both parents. Sam's mother and Pilar's father are dead, and Del was raised by his mother apart from his father. *Lone Star* is about the fulfillment of forbidden desires, but the desire is not for the parent of the opposite gender.

The next scene returns us to Pilar, but more importantly, to history writ large. Teachers and parents are at school discussing the teaching of history. Anglo parents are complaining that teachers are not teaching the standard curriculum, "tearin' everything down! Tearin' down our heritage, tearin' down our history, tearin' down the memory of people who fought and died for this land." A Chicano man interrupts, "We fought and died for this land, too," and an Anglo man responds, "Yeah, but you lost, buddy! Winners get bragging rights, that's how it goes." The principal intervenes, saying that it would be better to not think of it as a matter of winners and losers. In Texas, however, that's difficult because the Alamo, the great symbol of the war against Mexico, is regarded not mainly as an historical site, but as a nationalist shrine. The Anglo man invokes that history, when he asserts, "The men who founded this state have the right to have their story." He's interrupted by Danny (Jesse Borrego), a reporter for the local paper, who observes, "The men who founded this state broke from Mexico because they needed slavery to be legal to make a fortune in the cotton business!" Pilar offers that that is an oversimplification, but the Anglo man retorts, "You may call it history, but I call it propaganda." One of the teachers says that they are just "presenting a more complete picture," to which the Anglo mother responds, "And that's what's got to stop!" That last line, I think, suggests

Sayles's sympathy with multiculturalism. Sayles has said that he was thinking of the war in the former Yugoslavia when he was writing *Men with Guns* (a project that predates *Lone Star*), where one can see the result of the radical rejection of multiculturalism (Carson in Carson, *Interviews* 225). Sayles's acceptance of that paradigm is diametrically opposed to Bould, who condemns multiculturalism in a quote from Slavoj Žižek as merely "racism with a distance" (138). Bould's view of *Lone Star* derives directly from the 1970s critique of realism, condemning the "omniscience of the filmic narration . . . which announces itself as occupying a position divorced from the world it depicts," a stance which he likens to multiculturalism (142). But if this critique is at least consistent with poststructuralism, it's not clear how it can coexist with Bould's Marxism.

The conversation between parents and teachers makes plain why public history matters. The Chicano and Anglo communities have different versions of the story about the birth of Texas, just as we see that different characters have different versions of the more private history of events in Frontera. The identities of both communities are invested in these stories. Sayles does not pretend to be unbiased in presenting this meeting. The Chicano contingent comes off much more persuasively, and Danny's point about how a supposed war for freedom was actually motivated by the desire to make slavery legal (as it was not in Mexico) is a powerful and unfamiliar interpretation. In his conversation with Howard Zinn, Sayles says that the scene was inspired by the fact that because of its size, Texas has inordinate influence in the making of textbooks, and that "there was an extreme conservative husband and wife team who had the power to shape what history textbooks were used across the nation" (Neff 26). As an example of their extremity, this couple, the Gablers, recently managed to get Thomas Jefferson's role in American history demoted in Texas textbooks. The textbook meeting as a whole reveals Sayles's view that history is always told from one perspective or another, and, as the Anglo's intervention suggests, the only perspective normally heard is that of the "winners," the dominant group or class.

The county jail becomes the point where the several narrative strands of *Lone Star* come into contact. Sam and his deputies are investigating the shooting at Big O's, while Pilar comes in because she has heard her son has been picked up. Sam helps Pilar get Amado out of jail, and it becomes clear that there was something between them in high school, that Sam at least is interested in rekindling. A Hollywood montage shows us the forensic examination of the remains found in the opening scene, and it concludes with the badge being pulled from a beaker, now clearly reading Sheriff, Rio County. As we suspected, the dead man is Charlie Wade, and, while no cause of death can be determined, it is clear he was murdered. Although the murder is not officially Sam's to investigate, he does so knowing that his father is the prime suspect. His investigation is thus motivated by a quest to discover his own identity, and it turns out to tell him much more than who killed Charlie Wade.

But Sam Deeds is not the only one who does not know who he is. Neither does Pilar, nor her mother Mercedes, nor Del. Otis Payne seems more confident in his identity, but he has made considerable effort to make connections to his history. In a room off his bar, he has created a little museum devoted to black Seminoles, who successfully fought General Zachary Taylor in Florida, moved to Mexico to fight with Santa Anna, and finally went to Texas after the Civil War where they served as scouts for the U.S. Army. These ancestors represent the deep interconnections of the peoples of this region; their mixed blood foreshadows the film's final revelation, as they also seem to predict Del's career. But when Chet asks Otis if he is part Indian, Otis responds, "By Blood you are. But blood only means what you let it." In other words, identity does not reside in one's genes. What is important about *Lone Star* is its recognition that "identity" in the cultural sense cannot be divorced from the personal identity with which individuals must struggle. The film shows that politics without identity would not be human politics.

Del, unlike most other characters in the film, seems unconcerned about his own identity, being confident that he has been defined by his career and perhaps his mother. His father moved out when was eight years old to live with his mother's best friend just a few houses away. He pays a visit to his father only on official business after the soldier is shot. While he asks Otis a personal question or two, he remains distant, acting the part of the straight-arrow officer. Later though, he pays a call at Otis's home, where his current woman, Carolyn (Carmen De Lavallade), shows him what she calls Otis's "shrine," a collection of framed newspaper clippings about Del. He is surprised because his mother had told him his father never asked about his son. Later, we see Del tell Chet that they will invite his grandfather over for a barbecue. Del's new awareness of his father's love seems to cause him to see Chet as someone different from him and no longer a person simple to be pushed to follow his example.

Mercedes's attitude toward her heritage might be seen as the opposite of Otis's. She makes a point of her lack of connection to Mexico, calling her ancestors "Spanish," and insisting that her Mexican workers speak to her in English, since they are in America now. Early in the film, she sees some recent arrivals just out of the river run through her yard, and she calls the border patrol. Later, however, her employee Enrique (Richard Coca) appeals for her help when a woman he has been helping to cross the river has broken her leg. Mercedes at first threatens to call the authorities, but then we see a bit of her history, the night when she crossed river in the same way and met Eladio Cruz (Gilbert R. Cuellar Jr.). The memory softens her, and she drives the woman to a friend who was trained as a doctor and who owes her some favors.

Identity problems are portrayed as endemic to the world of *Lone Star*, and they are chronic rather than acute. What we have come to call "identity politics" is one of *Lone Star*'s major concerns, but unlike many discussions of that topic, it takes "identity" seriously, which it deals with at the intersection of the cultural and the personal. The problems of cultural identity are repeatedly discussed in the film. Frontera is multicultural, and it always has been, even though traditionally the different cultures seem to exist only in hierarchical relation to each other. The school meeting and another scene where we see Pilar actually teaching history instance the difficult change to the acceptance of an equality of cultures. Charlie Wade has stood for a rigid hierarchy enforced by violence, while Buddy represented a softer approach that still assumed the continuation of the status quo. The film's one living voice of unreconstructed racism, the bartender Cody (Leo Burmester), tells Sam that "to run a successful civilization you got to have lines of demarcation between right and wrong, this one and that one—your Daddy understood that." He then points out an interracial couple in the corner booth, and says that Buddy would have warned them "as kind of safety tip." The couple is Cliff and Priscilla (LaTanya Richardson), both noncommissioned officers, who are discussing getting married. Later, Cliff tells Mikey that Priscilla's family think any unmarried woman over thirty must be a lesbian, so they will accept her marrying a white man, and he responds, "Always heart-warming to see a prejudice defeated by a deeper prejudice." Cliff and Priscilla's relationship, even if it is still not completely accepted by everyone, shows that things have changed. It also anticipates *Lone Star*'s conclusion.

The issue of "lines of demarcation" comes up again when Sam goes to visit Chucho Montoya (Tony Amendola) across the border in Mexico. Montoya had lived in the United States for some years, but returned to Mexico to start a tire business. When Sam starts asking him questions, he draws a line in the sand and asks Sam to step across it, a representation of the border. Once Sam steps across he becomes the sheriff of nothing. After asserting his right on that basis not to answer his questions about Eladio Cruz, a man Sam has heard Charlie Wade murdered, Montoya remarks that birds and rattlesnakes take no notice of the line, so why should people? When Sam objects that the Mexican government has been happy to have the line, Montoya responds, "My government can go fuck itself, an so can yours. I'm talking about people here—men."

The theme of the border has been of even greater interest to academic readers of *Lone Star* than the Oedipal has been. As José Limón and Amy Kaminsky note, there is a long history of border novels and films on which *Lone Star* implicitly comments. Some of these films, such as *Touch of Evil* (Orson Wells, 1958) and *The Ballad of Gregorio Cortez* (Robert M. Young, 1982), Sayles says influenced *Lone Star* (West and West, in Carson, *Interviews* 212). Alan Barr observes that American culture's traditional concern with the "frontier" had long made borders an issue (365–66). Scholars have often recognized *Lone Star* as making some of the same points as cultural studies itself about the "liminality" of borders and the hybridity of cultures, as Cordelia Berrera's article illustrates. Rosa Linda Fregoso observes, "*Lone Star* reads like an application of Chicana/o borderlands theory" ("Imagining" 139). Kaminsky sees Sayles as correcting the overly positive connotations that the idea of the border has sometimes had in border theory (94). Jack Ryan says that *Lone Star* is about "the rifts caused by arbitrary boarders drawn between people and cultures" (175), which is exactly the point Montoya made to Sam.

Montoya then takes us back to history: "*Mi Amigo* Eladio Cruz is giving some friends of his a lift one day. . . ." The camera pans to the left and we see an isolated bridge, on which an old truck is stopped, and a man is changing a tire. A young Chucho gets out of back of the truck to relieve himself, though he is cautioned against it. We see a police car coming over the rise and it stops on the bridge. Charlie Wade and young Hollis get out and approach the truck. Wade seems friendly at first, but he indirectly accuses the driver of transporting "wetbacks" without cutting him in. When the man identifies himself as Eladio Cruz, Wade tricks him into getting his shotgun out of the cab and shoots him in cold blood. The scene ends when the camera pans up from Chucho, who has watched the murder from under the bridge, to Sam standing on it looking off into the distance. We now know that Wade, who had killed numerous men "resisting arrest," was not just trigger-happy, but someone who routinely committed murder in the service of his own power and interests.

Sam's investigation takes him to visit an old army friend of Buddy's, who casually lets slip that his father had a long-lasting affair while he was married to Sam's mother. Sam then goes to see his ex-wife, Bunny (Frances McDormand), where we get a sense of their radical incompatibility. While Sam is laconic and closed-mouth, she is manic in both behavior and speech. Her world is defined by football, something Sam has no interest in. While she displays some hostility to him, he is gracious to her, twice telling her that she looks good, though she does not seem so to us. Being her husband and working for her father is for Sam a negative identity, a role he has tried and rejected, but the conversation also suggests that he didn't try very hard. He visits Bunny because he has left some stuff in her garage, including things he inherited from his father. Among those papers, he finds a letter that tells him who his father's mistress was.

In the film's penultimate scene, Sam goes to O's late at night after knocking on Hollis's door and not finding him at home. Hollis and Otis are seated at the bar, though the place is closed. Sam tells them that Buddy killed Charlie and that he thinks the both of them were there in what was then Roderick's place when it happened. This time Otis begins to tell the story, which we see happen but we do not hear, because the action takes place against rhythm-and-blues music without audible dialogue. Charlie and Hollis come into the bar before young Otis expected them, and they find him dealing a poker game in the backroom.

Charlie kicks over the table and then repeatedly kicks young Otis, before ordering him at gunpoint to get the money they were expecting. He then points to another box behind the bar in which young Otis finds a handgun. As he puts his hand on it, Charlie turns to Hollis and winks. But as he turns back to shoot Otis, the music stops and we hear Buddy's voice say "Charlie Wade" and then see a gun shoot as Charlie falls dead over the bar. There's a reverse shot of Buddy walking toward us, and we assume he has done the shooting until the camera pulls back to reveal young Hollis holding the gun. The three of them bury Charlie on the old rifle range, and Buddy takes $10,000 from the office safe to make it look like Charlie had run off. He gives the money to Eladio Cruz's widow, Mercedes, as a kind of compensation for her loss, but it would be a few more years before she would become Buddy's lover.

The scene does what we expect the conclusion of a murder mystery to do, explain how the murder was committed by someone we did not expect and why he did it. But the scene does this unusually economically and entertainingly, and it does much more than this. While the movie has told a complicated story, by this point, few words are required to explain what happened. We get to see justice done, as Charlie dies trying to kill yet another man in cold blood. Sam recognizes that fact, and he agrees that there is no reason to make what the two older men have told him public. The scene brings together all three of the film's narrative threads, as we now know that Del exists only because of Hollis's action, and we now know that Buddy was involved with Pilar's mother. The full import of that knowledge, however, doesn't become clear until the final scene.

As Sam has been investigating Wade's murder, he and Pilar have become lovers. We have seen their history as lovers in high school, including Buddy rousting them half-dressed out of a car at the drive-in, and we know that they were forbidden to see each other afterward. We have heard Sam confess that the reason he came back to Frontera was because Pilar was there. The scenes between them have been full of romantic music drawn from the period of their youth, and the beginning of this renewed relationship is shot in slow, dreamy dissolves like those Sayles used on the "I'm On Fire" video. We have been made to believe that these people are right for each other. Pilar asserted earlier to her colleague, "Nobody stays in love for 26 years," but the film suggests otherwise, an affirmation of love unlike any other in Sayles's oeuvre.

In the film's concluding scene, we see Sam sitting on the hood of his car at a drive-in theater, now abandoned, staring at the blank, deteriorating white screen. Pilar joins him, and he asks her how long before she was born did her father die. She says, a couple of months, and he says, "Try a year and half." He hands her a picture of Buddy with his arm around young Mercedes, both smiling broadly. Sam tells her that Buddy bought the café for her mother, and that he paid the hospital bill when Pilar was born. The circle the film opened at the beginning is now closed, with Sam and Pilar being half-siblings. Pilar thinks that this must mean the end of their love, but she pleads that she can't have any more children. Sam tells her that if he met her for the first time that day, he would want to be with her. As she takes his hand, she says, "Forget the Alamo." There's a cut to a long shot of the two holding hands in front of the white screen, and we hear the bouncy "I Want to Be a Cowboy's Sweetheart" as the credits role.

Sayles has said of this ending that it is meant to show the isolation these two have chosen by choosing each other in opposition to social taboos against ethnic exogamy and incest (Smith 219). But the film actually does not establish that message very firmly. We have already seen a happy interracial couple, and Sam and Mercedes' widely known illicit relationship did neither of them any harm. It is true that incest is a bigger taboo than miscegenation, but it's not clear that the community knows they are brother and sister. The ending of *Lone Star*, then, is emotionally satisfying in a way that most of Sayles's endings are not. Here, the characters get what they want, and what they want fulfills one of those deep, repressed wishes Freud says all of us have experienced. Though my undergraduates often find this conclusion "icky," more mature, self-aware viewers often find it much happier than Sayles's comments on the film suggest he intended them to feel.

Some academic critics, however, have seen the ending, like the film as whole, as an allegory, as Fregoso explicitly does when she claims that *Lone Star* follows the patriarchal tradition of engendering the nation as female ("Imagining" 145).[5] Curiously she seems to ignore the fact that Pilar's sterility means she can't be fruitful and multiply. DuCille, while agreeing with Fregoso's general interpretation has the opposite complaint, that Pilar's sterility implies that nothing can change. While I admit that the mythic resonances of *Lone Star* invite such allegorizing,

I think this reading confuses Sayles's recognition of the limitations of individual action for a statement about what should or will happen in the future. We should read Pilar's sterility as Sayles's way of making their private arrangement morally unproblematic. But critics like Fregoso are unwilling to give Sayles the benefit of the doubt, and they insist on reading the film symptomatically. Disregarding the narratives of Pilar and Del, Fregoso holds that since the film centers on a white man's relationship to his father, "despite its overture to multiculturalism, the film's narrative is, on closer inspection, driven by a deeply colonialist and phallocentric project" ("Imagining" 141). Katherine Sugg similarly believes that it "fosters a discourse of cultural (as racial/biological) sameness and kinship that renders 'a new social order' on the border all the more possible, and profitable, for Anglo men" (125). This reading has been questioned quite persuasively by Handley, who argues that Fregoso's view "falls victim to [its] own determinism, insisting that Sam's power and authority is not different from his father's," when "Sam shows no interest in maintaining power" (180, n. 15).

Lone Star is Sayles's most popular film, and I think it is so because it gives audiences more of the wish fulfillment they typically get from Hollywood. This is true despite the film's critical realism, which is evident both in the mise en scene, and in the picture of Frontera's politics, past and present. But this realism exists side by side with a mythic level of meaning that lies not in the film's connection to the mystery genre, but rather in its use of conventions that structure several of the greatest works of twentieth-century American fiction, Fitzgerald's *The Great Gatsby* and William Faulkner's *Absalom, Absalom.* Each of these novels tells the story of a legendary figure, Jay Gatsby and Thomas Sutpen, respectively, but frames the story in terms of the narrators' perspective on it. Faulkner's novel is an especially clear precedent, because it involves the solution to a historical mystery, which its two narrators, Quinton and Shreve, must piece together. But in both novels, the narrators learn important things about themselves as they tell their stories. Like Sam, Fitzgerald's Nick decides to opt out of the world he has just made so vivid for us.

But the mythic dimension of *Lone Star* is not restricted to its evocation of dead giants. It is also a film that, uncharacteristically for Sayles, works very much at the level of the unconscious. For example, every significant event in the film seems to be doubled or even tripled. While at the level of the real we see the differences in the three cultures featured in the film, at the deeper level, events in each culture repeat those found in the others. One is reminded of John T. Irwin's study of Faulkner, *Doubling and Incest, Repetition and Revenge*, which finds in the great modernist's work the structures of the detective story, except that in Faulkner, as if illustrating Freud's theory of the compulsion to repeat, these structures are nearly always tragic.[6] In *Lone Star*, they have a comic resolution, even if it is one that does not portend genuine social renewal. But love in Hollywood comedies had become a more or less private matter at least as early as the 1930s.

The film's story results in several of the characters knowing better who they are, but it does not lead to any general solution for the larger identity troubles it portrays. Although it is consistent with Sayles's work in not claiming to be able to solve the social conflicts it represents, it is atypical in its movement from the public to the private. Sam Deeds is a rare Sayles hero in a position of authority, but he lacks the power to fundamentally change the political situation in which he finds himself. He decides in the end, apparently, to opt out, to choose individual happiness outside the community and its politics. Robert Ray has suggested that the typical Hollywood story has it both ways: the satisfaction of an individual desire is presented as if it were the solution to the community's problems. Sayles makes no claim that Sam and Pilar's love will change Frontera, but the effect of this ending is that we forget Frontera just as we are asked to forget the Alamo.

The reviews for *Lone Star* were overwhelmingly positive. It drew raves from Roger Ebert, who called it Sayles's "best work yet," Elvis Mitchell in the *New York Times*, and both *Time* and *Newsweek*. Peter Travers in *Rolling Stone* commented on the "uncommonly fine performances," an observation worthy of note, since the complexity of story and style tend to obscure the very fine acting. One advantage *Lone Star* had over most of Sayles's previous films is the presence of more familiar faces. While there were no players who were box-office leaders, Kris Kristofferson and Frances McDormand had wide recognition, and Matthew McConaughey was on the very cusp of stardom. For Chris Cooper, this was a breakout role, earning him a consistent stream of roles in major productions, where he had previously survived on made-for-TV movies. His ability to display a range of emotion despite having to play a Texan not prone to articulating his feelings is striking. In addition to the strong notices, *Lone Star* enjoyed the support of Columbia Pictures, which distributed it through the Sony Pictures Classics division. Unlike most of Sayles's pictures, this one made it into multiplexes. As a result, it grossed more than $13 million, far more than any other film Sayles has made.

Men with Guns

Sayles had come up with the idea for *Men with Guns* around 1994, and had scouted locations in Mexico after finishing *Roan Inish*. The film was delayed in part because of the revolt in the Mexican state of Chiapas, one of the locations where Sayles hoped to shoot, but also because Sayles was not in a position to finance another film after having sunk a significant amount into his previous film. After *Lone Star*'s success and the income from several screenwriting commissions, Sayles returned to *Men with Guns*. As with *Roan Inish*, he began preproduction work on the film before having secured enough money to complete it. The studios had no interest in a film that would be primarily in Spanish and would not have recognizable names in the cast. Eventually, two individuals, Lou Gonda and Microsoft cofounder Paul Allen put up $1 million each, and later, Sony Pictures Classics bought North American distribution rights; IFC Productions, a division of the Independent Film Channel purchased TV rights. Although the budget of $2.5 million was small even by Sayles's standards, the money went farther in Mexico.

In *Men with Guns*, Sayles returns to the more overtly political material with which he was identified in the 1980s. His protagonist, Dr. Fuentes (Frederico Luppi), however, bears some similarity to *Lone Star*'s Sam Deeds, as Sayles notes in his introduction to the book containing the screenplays for the two films. Both are about "a lone man on a quest. As the main protagonist in each searches for their very personal resolution, they serve as guides for us into wider social and political arenas" (*Men with Guns* vii). But whereas *Lone Star* relied on the detective story and some of the lore of the old West to create a sense of familiarity for the viewer, *Men with Guns* does not have any immediately helpful generic associations. It is, finally, a road movie, but one that has more in common with *Deliverance* (John Boorman, 1972) than with most incarnations of that formula. Like James Dickey's suburban male tourists on a canoe trip in deepest Appalachia, Dr. Fuentes has no idea what he is in for when he decides to take his vacation visiting his former students in the mountains of an unnamed Latin American country. While Sam Deeds's journey brings him physically and psychically home again, Dr. Fuentes's takes him to places he could not have imagined, and from which he will not return.

Dr. Fuentes is first seen in his urban office giving a rectal exam to a general. Sayles has suggested that this shows his intimacy with the elites who are responsible for much of the horror Fuentes will witness on his journey (Smith 243). At that moment, the doctor has power over the general, who is in the humiliating pose of leaning over an examining table with his pants down. But as their conversation later suggests, Fuentes is too ignorant to use his power to any advantage. The general tells him as the appointment ends, "You're like a child, Humberto. The world is a savage place." In some way, though, the general counts on that innocence. He has earlier asserted that the guerrillas were only a rumor that the common people spread because they like drama. People like Fuentes consent to the world the generals make, not because they approve of it, but because they would rather not see it.

Fuentes is a liberal, and the film will suggest that liberalism has both strengths and weaknesses. Moreover, the film does not give us another perspective on its events superior to liberalism, which is part of its profoundly pessimistic vision. As a liberal, Fuentes believes that the government program in which he taught students to become doctors to serve indigenous communities was both genuinely meant to help the people and had in fact done so. His trip to the mountains is planned so that he can see for himself how these former students are doing in their work. He sees them as his legacy, his little bit of immortality, which must suffice since he believes in science and progress rather than God and heaven. What he will witness may be "progress" to the general or the capitalists who support him, but to a liberal humanitarian like the doctor, it is anything but.

Sayles says that he worked to make the setting for *Men with Guns* a nonspecific Latin American country in order to avoid having viewers discount the events as merely the kind of thing that would go on in

Guatemala or some other location that could be dismissed as especially backward. He hoped that the story would have universal resonance by revealing "a dynamic as old as human society—men who have weapons and are willing to use them have power over those who don't" (*Men with Guns* ix). Yet, it is hard, if you know something about the recent history of the region, not to see this as a movie about Guatemala, where genocide was carried out by the government against the Mayan Indians in the 1980s. Although those events are not widely known outside Guatemala, which is not even the third or fourth place that comes to mind in connection with the word *genocide*, most Americans do have a sense of Central America as the home of protracted civil wars. Sayles's point is not to support one side or another in those wars, but to show their consequences for noncombatants. *Men with Guns* is a much more unambiguous antiwar film than was *Matewan*, but it seems to offer little hope of ever stopping war. The problems this film reveals are both unimaginably horrible and utterly unameliorable within the terms it sets out. Dr. Fuentes, like his former students, is powerless to stop the killing, and the viewer feels equally helpless (see figure 13).

Figure 13. Dr. Fuentes (Frederico Luppi) with the handiwork of men with guns.

The Guatemalan civil war was brought to a formal end in 1996, just before *Men with Guns* was made. Sayles's film, therefore, could not have been an intervention in that conflict, though he might have chosen to try to publicize a relatively little known episode of recent history, which the U.S. government actually abetted through its support of the military rulers of that country. But it is also clear that Sayles did not want to make a movie that could be understood to take sides in a war. Although *Men with Guns* clearly attributes the worst of the atrocities to the government and its army, the guerrillas are also responsible for some crimes, including the murder of one of Fuentes's students. What is clear is that the indigenous civilians suffer the most from the war even though many of them have no direct stake in it.

Sayles shows the horrors of war in ways calculated not to make war seem exciting. The visual impact and narrative adventure of war has interfered in the antiwar messages of films since D. W. Griffith's *Hearts of the World* (1918). Viewers are drawn into the excitement of conflict, and that tends to blunt the emotional impact and rational import of the harm that the conflict causes. To some extent *Matewan*'s stance against violence is affected by this problem. *Men with Guns* shows no real combat. We hear from both sides that they fight each other, but what we see is mainly the aftermath of the army's attacks on unarmed civilians. We see the remains of villages that have been entirely destroyed. We see human remains, left unburied as a warning to the local population. Occasionally, Sayles give us flashbacks to the events themselves, where the emphasis is on violence against helpless individuals who are murdered or raped. But even these disturbing scenes are kept quite brief, and they are presented as occurring in the mind of Domingo (Damián Delgado), a deserter from the army. They are thus clearly marked as elements of his guilty conscience, which helps to define their meaning for the viewer as well.

Men with Guns clearly wants to show that this war is not good for the people regardless of the intentions of those who are fighting. Sayles may be primarily interested here, as he was in *Matewan*, in speaking to the Left. Joe Kenehan is a pacifist, but his argument to the miners is not that violence is wrong, but that it is a strategy doomed to failure. The miners don't listen, and, though they win a battle, they lose the war, as Kenehan predicted. The Marxist tradition, with its vision of revolution modeled on France in 1789, has long embraced armed struggle as necessary and heroic. At least since the 1960s and the cult of Che Guevara, the Left in the North has championed the guerrillas fighting repressive regimes in the South. Yet what have all of these wars accomplished? The one successful one, Castro's in Cuba, resulted in a regime Sayles depicts in his novel, *Los Gusanos*, as being nearly as bad as its predecessor. In every other case, armed struggle has failed to topple the ruling oligarchies, or bring about more democratic or egalitarian rule, but it has brought suffering and death to millions. *Men with Guns* suggests that there has to be a better way.

It does not, however, give us much of clue about what that way might be, or even much more than a faint glimmer of hope that it might be found. Fuentes's quest to find evidence of some good the students he trained might have done is repeatedly frustrated. Of the students in the class photo he keeps with him, he finds only one alive, Bravo, who has left the village he was serving because unlike Cienfuegos, another student in the program, he got a warning and quit. Fuentes found Bravo accidentally before leaving the city for his "vacation." He heads off in search of the others, starting with Cienfuegos, whom Bravo tells him to ask for an explanation about why the program had ended. But he finds that Cienfuegos is dead, and when he asks who killed him, the answer is "men with guns." He gets more or less the same answer with regard to each of the others, except for the one woman, Montoya. She is supposed to have gone to the hidden village, Cerca del Cielo. What Fuentes finds incredible at first is that government itself, which has paid for the training of these students, has regarded them as subversives. As the Sergeant puts it, "What other reason would an educated man live out here?"

As in most road movies, Fuentes encounters a number of other travelers, some of whom end up riding with the doctor. The first ones he meets are American tourists who ask him if the news they had read of atrocities in the region is true. He says that it is not, showing that the Americans are better informed about his country than is Fuentes. Fuentes will meet them several more times and even end up riding on tires taken from their stolen car. That occurs after the doctor has taken on Rabbit (Dan Rivera González), a homeless boy, as a passenger, and after they have been both robbed at gunpoint by Domingo, who then steals the tourists' car.

The tourists persist in their vacation despite this problem and the violence that rages around them, but Sayles describes these tourists, played by Mandy Patinkin and Kathryn Grody, as being like Teflon, because nothing that they encounter sticks with them (Smith 239). While Fuentes is enlightened by his journey, they seem to learn nothing, preferring to remain in the world described in their guidebooks. In particular, they are obsessed with stories of human sacrifice practiced by the pre-Columbian inhabitants of the region. Fuentes tells them that this was not true of the ancient peoples of his country, and later, the boy, Rabbit, explains that when he worked as a guide at ancient ruins he got bigger tips for making up stories about such rituals. Fuentes tells the tourists that "It was other tribes, attacking from the north," who practiced human sacrifice, a statement that points to the more recent role of the United States in the region. Sayles says that tourists represent "what America is to Central America—since the Monroe Doctrine, which basically said, 'Anything that goes on in this hemisphere, we want to control.' The United States has done many things in Latin America but none of them have been to make those people more self-sufficient" (Smith 239). Sayles is aware that the United States was involved in these Latin American civil wars, supplying cash to the side it favored and covertly arranging to topple governments of which it disapproved. But besides these veiled references, *Men with Guns* does not deal with the United States's role in the war it depicts.

The tourists' interest in ancient human sacrifice is, of course, ironic from their first mention of it, since humans are being sacrificed all around them. But the irony is deepened by a story that Padre Portillo (Damián Alcázar) tells about why he left the village where he had been the parish priest, which Sayles shows us a flashback. After the army had burned the villages above and below his, it came to his village and told the people that if they wanted to avoid the same fate, they had to execute five men and the priest. The village men get together to decide whether to fight, to run, or to comply with the commandante's order. They choose the last option, with even those who would die, including the priest, voting in favor of the sacrifice. The priest, however, runs away, and even though the villagers execute the five others, the army destroys the village anyway. We don't know whether the commandanté would have kept his word if the priest had been willing to sacrifice himself, though the priest says, "he failed the test." Although the incident seems too terrible and too perfect to be true, Sayles says on his DVD commentary that an incident like this had happened in Guatemala.

The people of this village were not supporting the guerrillas, and the priest, though he believes in liberation theology, merely wanted to help the people live better lives, both spiritually and materially. But like Fuentes's students, the very act of helping these Indians was threatening to government, which needed them to be a cheap source of labor for the rich landowners. Sayles presents self-sufficient subsistence agriculture as an alternative preferable to most others available in the region he is depicting, and he may be correct. But this view is consistent with the antimodernism that we saw in *Roan Inish*, and one is forced to wonder to what extent it is part of the message of *Men with Guns* as well. Sayles shows the people of this village practicing a kind of primitive communism and a kind of primitive democracy, in the face of government fascism. He clearly admires their sense of community and their bond with the land, and he depicts the willingness of their leaders to die for the village as heroic. The priest's actions, however, suggest that this is not a path that Europeans, even a Christian who used to have fantasies of martyrdom, are capable of following.

The priest finally does decide to sacrifice himself when the doctor's car is stopped at an army checkpoint, at this point seemingly surrendering out of guilt. As Fuentes sets out on the last leg of his journey, he has with him, not only Domingo and Rabbit, but Graciela (Tania Cruz). She was raped by soldiers and has been mute ever since. Fuentes talks her out of killing herself after she has made off with Domingo's revolver. The four of them set out on foot up a steep mountain through the jungle to find Cerca del Cielo. Even the guerrillas they encounter on their climb (and who treat them far better than the army soldiers they have met) do not know where the place is, or even if it exists. Fuentes hopes to find Montoya there, but when he finally arrives at the mountain encampment of refugees, she is not among them. He has completely failed in the mission he originally planned for the trip.

They find instead a woman we saw at the beginning of the film and on several occasions later, telling a story to her daughter about a doctor who sometimes has trouble breathing. Sayles says that he got the idea of this woman from reading magical-realist novels, where people often had paranormal powers that did them no practical good (Smith 242). This woman knows what will happen to Doctor Fuentes, but her ability to tell the future didn't keep her from stepping on a land mine. Her effect on the film seems to be to de-realize it slightly, to make it more mythic and universal than it might otherwise seem. The last time we see her, she tells her daughter that the doctor has come to stay. She's right in that Fuentes dies, but he does so before he can get the shrapnel out of her leg. Only after Fuentes's death does the film offer us some slight moments of redemption. Domingo hesitates but finally picks up the doctor's bag and goes to help the woman. Graciela looks up to higher mountains and sees perhaps the possibility of a better place on earth. But these glimmers seem awfully meager given what we have just witnessed.

Fuentes seems to be at peace with himself when he dies, and it is another of the film's ironies that Domingo represents the legacy that he hoped his students would be. Fuentes's dealings with Domingo might be seen as an illustration of pacifism in action. After Domingo robs the doctor and Rabbit, he returns in the tourists' car, wounded by a gunshot to the abdomen. With Domingo still holding a gun on him, Fuentes digs out the bullet and binds the man's wounds even though it is clear that Domingo could easily be overpowered. Later, the doctor discovers that the gun has no bullets, but instead of confronting Domingo, he uses the knowledge to his advantage, being now able to call Domingo's bluff. The doctor has plenty of chances to get away from the thief but does not. In the end, his example is our only way to account for Domingo's redemption. Fuentes's liberalism, then, is ignorant, but it is not in Sayles's conception wrong in the way that the more extreme political options are portrayed as being. This liberalism is not the same as that of the America tourists, who can never understand their government's role in the world. Sayles is not endorsing the status quo, but he is rejecting violence as a failed means of transformation.

Given the disturbing and unhopeful tenor of this film, and the fact that non–Spanish-speaking Americans required subtitles to understand all but a few lines of its dialogue, it is not surprising that *Men with Guns* did not repeat the commercial success of *Lone Star*. The film got good reviews from high-profile critics such as Janet Maslin and Roger Ebert, and even the more negative reviews were in general respectful. Stanley Kauffmann, a longtime Sayles naysayer, gave the film a surprisingly positive review, though he, like a number of critics, hated the ending's epiphanies. But the film was reviewed in fewer places than many of his others, and it has been suggested that the distributor put its efforts behind a contemporary release, David Mamet's *The Spanish Prisoner* (Molyneaux 244). All of this added up to Sayles's lowest U.S. gross to that point, a mere $750,000.

Limbo

> "When people start into a story they have to see the end or they aren't happy."
>
> —Mother, *Men with Guns*

Despite the commercial difficulties of *Men with Guns*, Sony Pictures, the parent of Columbia, remained interested in Sayles. Prior to his last picture, he had made a string of profitable movies on small budgets. By the late 1990s, very few of the independent distributors from the 1980s such as Cinecom were still in business, and most independent films were now being distributed by subsidiaries of major studios, more of which were being created each year. Sony made a deal with producers Maggie Renzi and Sarah Green (who worked with David Mamet), giving the company "first look" rights in return for office space and other expenses. The deal specified films with budgets up to $8 million, which is what Sayles got to make *Limbo*, the first project for Green/Renzi. The film would be distributed by Columbia's revived Screen Gems division, which used to be the firm's television arm. This was the biggest budget Sayles had yet worked with, but he still had far less than the industry average, which in 1999 was more than $50 million. Still, Sayles was able to make a movie that looks anything but low budget, partly because he reunited here with cinematographer Haskell Wexler, and partly because after all these years, as *Lone Star* proved, Sayles had learned how to make great-looking pictures for little money.

The place to begin to talk about *Limbo* is with its ending, its most famous (or notorious) feature. The film's three main characters, Joe Gastineau (David Strathairn), Donna De Angelo (Mary Elizabeth Mastrantonio), and her daughter, Noelle (Vanessa Martinez), have been stranded on an island in the Alaskan wilderness, and in the last scene they are waiting to learn whether the airplane that is landing in front of them will mean rescue or death. But rather than let us know which it is, Sayles fades to white. It is a radical violation of audience expectations, and it is important to explain why. Sayles's films characteristically end without "closure," without tying up all of the loose ends, without suggesting that everyone will live happily (or miserably) ever after. Feminist and other film theorists of the 1970s and 1980s used to complain about the closure typical of popular narratives in general, and especially of studio-era Hollywood cinema, the characteristic happy endings that papered over all kinds of unresolved problems and conflicts. It was argued that women liked narratives such as soap operas, which avoid closure simply by not ending. But what Sayles does in *Limbo* is not best understood as avoiding closure. Had he simply wanted that, he could have left the characters on the island with various possibilities still open: they might be rescued; they might survive in wilderness; they might die of exposure; they might be murdered.

Rather, Sayles teases the audience by setting up an either/or question. It is as if David Selznick decided to end *Gone with the Wind* before Rhett says his famous exit line. As it is, *Gone with the Wind* permits viewers to impose their own closure, to decide whether Rhett and Scarlett's relationship is finished, or whether she will get him back "another day." Without the final lines, viewers would still be free to do this, but they would find it harder because an episode in the lives of the characters was left in the middle. The contract that a storyteller normally works under is that he or she will "finish" the story. That does not mean, necessarily, that "closure" will be provided. Lots of stories end with lines like, "and no one ever heard from Amelia again" or "and the ship has never been found." Narratives that end this way lack traditional closure, and instead leave the audience with a mystery, which the narrator shares with them. What Sayles seems to be saying on the contrary is, I know what happened to them, but I'm not going to tell you.

There is only one other narrative I can think of that ends the way Sayles ended *Limbo*, and since it came later, perhaps Sayles's film was an influence. *The Sopranos* ended its six-year run with Tony and his family sitting in a diner and the suggestion that a hit man may be about to strike with a fade to black. As with *Limbo*, but on a much larger scale, critics and viewers complained loudly. Had David Chase merely wanted to avoid closure, he could have left the story where it was in the middle of the episode: a war with rival boss Phil Leotardo is in progress, and we don't know how it will come out. As it is, the storyteller seems to be deliberately withholding information. The tactic may be less of a surprise in a narrative like the Sopranos, since suspense had been one of its frequent modes. Moreover, while there is no accepted formula for ending a long-running television series, feature films have traditionally entailed the expectation of an ending.

It has been said that Sayles's ending is in fact revealed in the film's title, but Sayles does not see it that way. To him, *limbo*, a term borrowed from Catholic theology where it means the place reserved in the afterlife for the virtuous but unbaptized, is a state into which many people fall when they are unhappy but afraid to do anything to change their lives, putting up with a bad marriage or a hated job, because it is too much of a risk to let go of them (West and West, "Not Playing"). Joe and Donna are both depicted as taking risks to get out of the limbo they have been stuck in. But "limbo" is mentioned in the film only by Noelle when she is inventing lines from a diary found at the abandoned cabin in which they find shelter. She says that the diarist's father, who brought his family to the island to raise foxes for fur, calls the island "Limbo" because, "it sure isn't heaven, it's too cold to be hell, and it's not purgatory, because that has an end." Sayles's characters are not finally in limbo, since their stay on the island will end one way or the other. Sayles chose not to leave them there, but rather to leave us hanging.

Sayles has seldom been called visually innovative, and he has abjured style as an end in itself. But he has consistently been an innovative storyteller. Not only do his films avoid the confines of Hollywood genres, but they also often entail narrative strategies that are unusual in any medium. And while Sayles does not make movies about movies, *Limbo* was his fourth film in succession to be about storytelling. There are at least four different kinds of stories represented within the film's larger narrative. There are commercial stories, designed in this case to sell Alaska to tourists, including both the opening video about the state and also a tour guide's spiel in the bar. There are personal stories, like the ones Donna and Joe tell each other, which are designed to reveal, but also to conceal, the self from an intimate. There are the stories that the local bar patrons tell each other, which are what Joan Didion was referring to when she observed that "we tell ourselves stories in order to live." These are stories of local history, personal disasters, and occasional triumph that define who these people are—nonfiction stories—which is not to say that they are the whole truth or without even some deliberate falsification, but that they are taken to be more or less truthful. The last type of story is fiction, such as Noelle invents, and that type is the most like what Sayles is doing in the film as a whole. The first of Noelle's stories, about a baby born with gills, is one the director actually wrote in high school (DVD commentary). Her continuation of the diary instances the way fiction can reveal deeper realities than attempting to tell the facts.

Sayles's meditation on storytelling should make us aware of his interest in narrative form. With the ending of the film, he has created an innovation in storytelling, which may have been inspired by the idea of the diary. Diaries characteristically don't end; they just break off. They are by the usual standards, deficient narratives. The clairvoyant Mother in *Men with Guns* comments that people are happy only when they see the end of a story from the beginning. Sayles has said of *Limbo* that, "we are asking the audience to really take the same trip that the characters are, and that trip entails surprise and risk. I think the most important phrase in the movie is when the developer says, 'What do you get when you get on a roller coaster? You get the illusion of risk, not real risk.' Most genre movies—and I write them for other people—are the illusion of risk." (West and West, "Not Playing"). The risk that the audience runs is that the ending they think they see when the movie starts will not come about.

Sayles has said that the only other film that shifts genres as radically as *Limbo* is Jonathan Demme's *Something Wild* (1986, a film in which Sayles had a cameo role), "which starts out as a screwball comedy and ends up as a thriller" (West and West, "Not Playing"). Sayles's film is actually the more radical of the two. The two genres *Something Wild* combines had been combined before, albeit in different forms, by, among other people, Alfred Hitchcock in *North by Northwest* (1959). The shocks in *Limbo* are smaller than the ones in *Something Wild*, but they are more surprising. *Something Wild* begins with mild transgressions and shifts to violent ones. *Limbo* begins with ordinary reality, and it shifts to an extreme predicament toward which the filmmaker has previously hinted only in the most oblique ways.

Limbo for more than an hour of its running time seems to be among Sayles's most conventionally realist works, and in many respects, among his best. The opening sequence, shot first on video and made into a kinescope, is a sort of mock travelogue, like something that a government tourist office might produce. While the narrator talks about the risks that have been taken in the past by fisherman, loggers, prospectors, and others, the images show us an Alaska full of cruise ships, tourists, stuffed rather than wild animals, and an automated salmon-canning line. As we move into the film's narrative, the introductory narration is taken over by Harmon King (Leo Burmester), as we watch workers clean salmon by hand. Harmon's mock heroic monologue seems to set a comic tone for the film, though it is also serious commentary on the difficulties of earning a living in this place, and the images confirm his words.

Work continues to be the focus as the scene shifts to a wedding reception, where our focus is not on the guests, but on various people working at the reception. We meet Noelle serving hors d'oeuvres, Donna providing entertainment as the singer for a band, and Joe doing odd jobs including the delivery of wine. We also meet their employers, Frankie (Kathryn Grody) and Lou (Rita Taggart), a lesbian couple who run the inn where the reception is being held. Even the guests we overhear—father of the bride, Albright (Michael Laskin) and Phil—are talking about economic matters and the problem of keeping logging sites away from the sight lines of cruise ships.

Against this background, Donna and Joe meet, and that begins what is certainly Sayles's most well-developed intimate relationship. It is unusual in that both of the lovers are over forty, and both are working-class. As is characteristic of Sayles, the usual gender roles are modified: Donna is the more open, the willing risk-taker. Joe, while in many respects typically masculine, is romantically the more passive. They move from dancing warily around each other in the beginning to finding out that they belong together by enduring successfully the stress of being stranded in the wilderness. It is important to note that this story is completed, since we know that, whatever happens, Joe and Donna will be together.

The relationship becomes more complicated when it is revealed that Noelle had a crush on Joe beginning before her mother met him. The three of them form the Oedipal triangle many critics thought they saw in *Lone Star*. Because Noelle is female, it is also an unusual incarnation of a familiar narrative, and Noelle's creation of the diary will make its importance apparent by her introduction of a second male figure, a fox who comes to the diarist in a dream as a young man and, unlike all the other foxes, unpaired. Bringing the Oedipal pattern to the surface also reflects the trajectory of this film, which moves away from a focus on a specific social reality into the realm of mythic themes, which in addition to Oedipus include the human struggle with nature and the related question of risk.

The trajectory from mundane to mythic was in *Men with Guns* as well, but it was less jarring in the earlier film since Fuentes very quickly finds himself in the middle of a war, putting a quick end to the ordinary. This pattern tells us something about Sayles's oeuvre, which is that he has not been content to remain on the surface of things or to limit the reference of his films to a particular time or place. So at the same time that *Matewan* is very much about the West Virginia coalfields in 1920, it is also about the continuing difficulties of workers to find a successful response to the violence perpetrated against them by capital. *Limbo* is a detailed representation of southeastern Alaska as an economic and social reality, but it is also about the inherent precariousness of human existence. The continuum from the historical and social particular to the universally human is exactly what Lukács argued makes a novel realist. For him, characters needed to represent social types of the human, and those that were merely idiosyncratic, were less than real no matter how factual their existence might be. Thus, it would be a mistake to say that Sayles is less of a realist because he takes the narrative in the direction of the universal. There is, in fact, a rigorous realism about the film even as it shifts from the social world to the wilderness. The shift begins when Joe, Donna, and Noelle sail away on Joe's brother Bobby's boat. The women think it's just a pleasure cruise, and Joe believes that he's doing Bobby a favor by pretending to be his employee to impress clients. A pleasant sailing montage is first interrupted by the need to take shelter from a storm in the lee of an island. Only then does Joe—and the audience—learn that the trip was actually planned so that Bobby could meet some drug dealers whose goods he had thrown overboard on an earlier smuggling operation. In the next scene, after Joe had gone below to tell the women that they would need to leave the trip sooner than expected, we hear faint conversation from on deck, and then gunshots. We don't see the violence, and like Joe, we can only guess what has happened. We don't see the faces of the killers, either, as Sayles gives us only a brief glimpse of one's legs as he descends to the lower deck. We hear gunshots as the three swim away from the boat, but we don't see the shooters. Once we get to the island, the realism continues with an utter lack of any romanticism of nature. Although the photography earlier in the film had given us picture-postcard sort of landscapes, here we are immersed in a forbidding wilderness, the dimensions of which cannot be perceived. As Sayles put it, "The thesis of that treatment is that human beings are romantic about nature but nature is not romantic about human beings" (West and West, "Not Playing"). The stranded family is not the Swiss Family Robinson, and being stranded in Alaska is nothing like living at Walden Pond. This classical setting for a romance narrative thus both is and is not one. Instead of an alternative to society, life in this wilderness demonstrates its necessity, a universal that shows us why the particulars of the film's first half matter (see figure 14).

Sayles claims that genre films offer "the illusion of risk." This is in one sense a quite accurate account of the way conventional formulas

Figure 14. Donna (Mary Elizabeth Mastrantonio) and Joe (David Strathairn) await their fate in the wilderness.

work in fictions, whether in print and on the screen. We read each new mystery or romance, or see each new romantic comedy or action picture, knowing what the end will be, though we don't necessarily know how we will get to it. Hollywood movies have always relied heavily on formulas, and they probably do so more often today than in the studio era. There have always been films, however, that take viewers to some place unexpected, and these are not always art films or the work of self-conscious iconoclasts. Part of appeal of the original cycle of film noir was that its films were more likely to make the viewers' risk seem real. For example, the detective hero of *Out of the Past* (Jacques Tourneur, 1947) does not survive the film, despite his having reformed and having been our point of identification throughout. And yet, all a film or novel can ever give us is the illusion of risk, since, unlike the characters stranded in *Limbo*, we are not endangered. Moreover, risk is a matter of probability, not of outcome. If we compare, for example, two identical automobile trips, one completed safely and the second ending in an accident, the second is no less risky than the first. The ending of *Limbo* does not confirm the viewer's greater risk, but rather seems to show the filmmaker's desire to take advantage of his or her confidence in him. Sayles in making *Limbo* is a bit like Smilin' Jack Johannson (Kris Kristofferson): you like him, but you can't trust him.

Limbo was premiered as an official selection of the Cannes Film Festival in May 1999, the first time a Sayles film had been so honored. However, the film did not do well with critics at Cannes, and it didn't do much better a month later when it was released in the United States Predictably, critics focused on the film's lack of generic faithfulness, claiming that it made the film incoherent. The ending was often explicitly criticized as cheating the audience or copping out. The more perceptive critics noted the fine performances, the surprisingly (for Sayles) fluid editing, and the general effectiveness of the film's first hour or so. A few recognized the power of the scenes on the island, and a very few saw the ending as appropriate. Audiences seemed to agree that the film, as Andrew Sarris put it, "seems designed to punish us for becoming attached to the characters and the milieu" (*New York Observer*). *Limbo*'s U.S. gross was only about $2 million, returning the lowest percentage of its cost of any of Sayles's films until *Honeydripper*.

Millennial Sayles

Sayles's films after *Limbo* continue to explore new locations and subjects, but they tend to be less innovative in narrative structure, relying on patterns familiar either from Sayles's earlier work or film history. As the first decade of the twenty-first century progressed, Sayles had increasing trouble finding financing and distribution for his work. The independent movement that he helped launch was effectively over by 2004 if not earlier.

Sayles's next film, *Sunshine State*, came about because he couldn't find the Florida he had been looking for. He wanted to make a film based on his short story "Treasure," but the locations he hoped to use no longer existed. Since he was a child, Sayles has been a frequent visitor to Florida, and he was looking for "The small-town Florida I remembered." It "was gone, . . . swept away by corporate tourism" (Meyer, *San Francisco Chronicle*). "I drove from Everglades City all the way up to Pensacola. I hadn't been around there in over 10 years and it had changed so much I didn't feel we could afford to recreate what I remembered" (Ross, *Tampa Tribune*). Instead, he found Amelia Island and its American Beach, one of the few historically black beach communities on the East Coast. He created a new story about the changes in Florida he had witnessed, the island having enough of the old Florida to allow Sayles to depict the work of the very economic forces that had already changed most of the rest of the state. *Sunshine State* was produced solo by Maggie Renzi for Anarchist's Convention, Sayles's and Renzi's own production company, on a budget of $5.6 million. This was a step down from the funding level of his previous film, as was the distribution company, which was Sony Picture's Classics.

Sunshine State is a complex, multistoried mosaic like *City of Hope*, but it is also the closest thing Sayles has made to a comedy since *The Brother from Another Planet*. It is a fairly dark comedy, with one of the funny bits being the repeated inability of Earl Pinkney (Gordon Clapp) to commit suicide. Still, after *Men with Guns*, *Lone Star*, and *Limbo*, *Sunshine State* represents a considerable shift in tone, treating its material with a new lightness that will be continued in *Casa de los babys*. Both films feature sharp dialogue of the sort more often associated with

Woody Allen. While the object of Sayles's wit is often social and political, it is also invoked in conversations about personal life and love that one might find in Allen. And unlike in *City of Hope*, potentially melodramatic situations are treated ironically or comically. Where the earlier film seems to feature irreconcilable conflicts, *Sunshine State* focuses on characters who are at least beginning to solve their own problems.

There are four main plotlines, plus other characters thrown in to comment on or complicate them. They are set on Plantation Island, which includes the communities of Delrona Beach, an older resort town, and Lincoln Beach, a middle-class African American enclave. One story involves the return of Desiree Perry (Angela Bassett) to visit her mother, Eunice Stokes (Mary Alice), many years after she was sent away at fifteen to hide her pregnancy. A second story concerns Marly Temple (Edie Falco), a middle-aged woman running the hotel and restaurant her father, Furman (Ralph Waite), had built and run. Marly is ready to leave Delrona Beach, but her father doesn't want to sell the business. Plot number three involves Francine Pinkney (Mary Steenburgen), who is in charge of a local festival called "Buccaneer Days." Finally, the plot that brings into contact these and most of the more minor threads is about attempts by several real estate development firms, including the Exley Corporation, which already has a significant development on the island, to buy up land in the area to build gated communities and beachfront high rises.

The way that the stories and events of *Sunshine State* are juxtaposed seems designed to keep the viewer off balance, and at least sometimes to create ironic commentary. The film opens at night with a burning pirate ship, watched by a black adolescent, whom we later learn is Eunice's grandnephew, as a police car arrives. We won't learn the significance of this scene until later. The camera pans up to a black sky, and we here a voice offscreen say, "In the beginning there was nothing." There's a cut to a daytime scene of a golf foursome, consisting of Silent Sam (Eliot Asinof), Buster Bidwell (Clifton James), Jefferson Cash (Cullen Davis), and the speaker of the intro line, Murray Silver (Alan King) who is pontificating about how they had transformed Plantation Island (and by implication, Florida). Murray's remarks seem to be addressed mainly to Cash, the only non–senior citizen, who asks the questions the others answer. This foursome will appear several more times throughout the film, acting, as Sayles has said, more like Olympian gods than a Greek chorus (DVD commentary). They are the unseen decision makers who control most of our lives without our being aware of them. But, their honesty and irreverence also establish the lighter, more humorous tone, which must have been one of Sayles's motives in casting the comedian King as Murray.

As the relationship of these two scenes suggest, *Sunshine State* does not rely mainly on character "trades," as *City of Hope* did, to link its disparate plotlines. Since the location here is not a city, where people might normally walk past each other, such encounters would not be easy to stage. The shifts between stories are usually done with cuts, though in a few instances a single location is used to put the characters into some kind spatial relation to each other. Marly's restaurant serves that purpose near the beginning of the film. There Desiree and her husband, Reggie (James McDaniel), stop so that she can use the restroom, and Marly confronts Jack (Timothy Hutton) who has been "mentally undressing" the property from across the street, while his competition studies the place through binoculars from a pier somewhat further away. These scenes put characters into some kind of contact who will have little do with each other, such as Desiree and Marly, but also begin what will turn into a relationship between Marly and Jack and establish the corporate takeover plot.

In *Limbo*'s Alaska, Sayles had presented a tourist economy in the making, but Florida had long been dominated economically by tourism. What is happening here is that an economy that had been comprised of locally owned businesses is being transformed into one dominated by absentee corporations that turn the locals into employees. Dr. Lloyd (Bill Cobbs), a longtime leader of the Lincoln Beach community, explains what this means for it:

> Used to be if you were black, you'd buy black. Jim Crow days, you wanted your shoes shined or your laundry done, or a taxi ride to the train station you were on your own. You wanted some ribs, chicken, fish sandwich—chances are a black man owned the place you got it in. Now the drive-throughs will serve anybody, but who owns them? Not us—our people just wearing paper hats and dippin' fries out.

Sunshine State shows us is this same process happening to everyone in Delrona Beach. As capital becomes increasingly restricted to large corporations with headquarters in a few major cities, small towns increasingly have no genuinely local businesses and no real local bourgeoisie. The situation is bad not only for traditional small-business owners such as Furman, but also for the young, like his daughter or Terrell, whose ability to make things might have at one time given him a future. But we are also reminded that when Furman built his business, Jim Crow was the law, and African Americans did not have the opportunities that Desiree and her anesthesiologist husband have had.

The focus of *Sunshine State* is not the struggle between the local petit bourgeois and multinational capital, which we know the locals will lose sooner or later. Rather, the focus is on the experiences of different people living in the midst of this change. The emphasis is on their resiliency, rather than on their failures. Moreover, the past is not, Eunice and Dr. Lloyd's perspectives notwithstanding, represented nostalgically. Both Marly and Desiree's families have experienced tragedy: Marly lost her older twin brothers to an auto accident when they were still in high school and Desiree was sent away from home at fifteen to bear a stillborn child. Terrell (Alex Lewis), the boy we saw watching the ship burn, is living with Eunice because his father, under the influence of drugs, killed his mother and himself. Sayles is interested in the way that the different characters respond to changing circumstances. For Marly, the developer's interest in her property will make it possible for her to escape. Terrell's presence in her mother's house gives Desiree a reason to want to stay for more than a few days.

And it's not just personal histories about which the film will refuse to be nostalgic. Francine's efforts to stage Buccaneer Days lead her to comment on the way history has to be fictionalized in order to make it commercially viable in tourism. She complains to her husband, "People think that it's just there, like Christmas or Thanksgiving. They don't appreciate how difficult it is to invent a tradition." An earlier conversation between Exley spokesman Todd Northrup (Sam McMurray) and Francine has already explained why inventing a tradition is necessary:

> NORTHRUP: "But you've got history to burn."
> FRANCINE: "People hate history."
> NORTHRUP: "Indians, pirates, Spanish gold, the plantation thing."
> FRANCINE: "Mass murder, rape, slavery—"
> NORTHRUP: "Hey—Disnify it a little and they'll come back for more."

Francine here reveals the pre–twentieth-century history of Florida, and it's not pirates she's talking about. In fact, compared to the Spanish and English, colonizers, slave traders, and plantation owners, the pirates actually look like the better alternative. In a speech in his screenplay that got cut from the film, Sayles has an academic at a booth at the mall give a little lecture explaining that the native Timucuas fought with the Spanish, but, "The British report that they massacred a large group of Christianized Indians in a Franciscan mission on this island in the late 1600s" (*Sunshine State* screenplay 250). Sayles might have found a way to point out that the pirate ships were "democratic in an undemocratic age," and that they were multiracial and even sometimes included women as equals (Linebaugh and Rediker 162). In Buccaneer Days, the pirate seems to be something like the Western outlaw, a mythic figure inspiring both fear and envy.

More recent Florida history is left to Murray and his golfing buddies, whose version of it suggests that fiction has always been key to the region's prosperity under capitalism. They developed Plantation Island by turning something worse than swampland, inhabited chiefly by alligators and mosquitoes, into something profitable: a dream. According to Murray, "you don't sell land. I mean what is land—a patch of dirt, a tree maybe—who cares? . . . A dream is what you sell, a concept. You sell sunshine, you sell orange groves, you sell gentle breezes wafting through the palm tress." The palm trees, which are not native to the area, existed only in the brochure. This history is, of course, not at all part of Buccaneer Days, which is actually a continuation of the sort of fiction Murray is talking about. At the end of the film, though, he ties recent history to ancient, saying "Before it was land it was gold," and telling the story about how the Spaniards worked Indians to death trying to find gold in Florida after seeing one of them wearing a gold necklace. When none was found, it was determined that the jewelry washed ashore from a Spanish galleon on its way back from South America.

Murray comments not only on history, but also on the environment that his development created, which he calls "nature on a leash." We see some of this version of nature in *Sunshine State*, but we see other images as well. These range from pristine beaches and a canoe outing on a beautiful and natural river, to the ugly commercial strip near the restaurant and motel, and even to a pulp mill. Marly's mother, Delia

(Jane Alexander) is the film's chief environmental advocate. Like the other conflicts in the film, the argument over environmental preservation is not resolved. There is hope because people holding Delia's views hardly existed when Murray and company began their work, and in the end, because she turns out to understand the larger economic picture, it looks like she might be able to use profits from the sale of the motel to benefit her cause. In a later scene, after the foursome has discussed global warming, Murray asserts, "Nature is overrated," to which Silent Sam replies, "But we will miss it when it's gone" (see figure 15). Perhaps the best that *Sunshine State* can offer us is that we might be able to keep it around a bit longer.

Nothing ends too badly for the characters in this film, and, indeed, the worst outcome pertains to the Exley Corporation, which has to suspend its new development because apparently ancient human remains are found as construction begins. The disruption is almost certainly only temporary, but it means that Jack has to leave the island before he and Marly can get to know each other well enough. We know, however, that she can look forward to the freedom to move on herself. Desiree and her mother have not quite forgiven each other, but they have talked enough to begin to reestablish a relationship. Even Earl, who has been embezzling money from the bank that employs him, seems to have obtained

Figure 15. The "Gods" play golf in the "paradise" they have created.

enough cash from a bribe by land developers to pay back the missing funds. And his wife, Francine, who is near collapse after the trials of the festival, now needs him. Hopeful outcomes are not guaranteed, but merely suggested. Like most of Sayles's work, *Sunshine State* ends without closure. The final scene, in which we find Murray's foursome golfing on a grassy median in the middle of fast-food strip, is a sight gag that restages the central economic and environmental conflicts that the film has presented.

The reviewers were certainly kinder to *Sunshine State* than they had been to *Limbo*, with the majority of critics giving the film positive notices and none of the major ones being any worse than mixed. But the film didn't seem to excite many critics, and reviews often remarked that it was not one of Sayles's best. The performances of Edie Falco, Angela Bassett, and Mary Alice were widely praised, but the fine acting of the cast as a whole was less often noticed. Many critics, including those who had previously been generally supportive of Sayles, felt that the film didn't quite hang together. As usual, some critics saw Sayles's social observation as "didactic," while others praised him for keeping it to the background. The film's box-office numbers suggest a similarly mixed reaction among viewers. The film earned only about a $3 million U.S. gross, only slightly more than 50 percent of its cost.

Casa de los babys

While Sayles was in Mexico making *Men with Guns*, he was inspired to write another screenplay for a film that he would shoot in that country. After *Sunshine State*, Sayles and Renzi had hoped to make a film about a Scottish Highlander who's defeated at the Battle of Culloden, sold into slavery in the colonies and ends up at the Battle of Quebec in the middle of the French and Indian War. They needed about $25 million to make this period piece, and, while Renzi was trying to raise that sum, Sayles went to Mexico to make *Casa de los babys*. A distribution deal including some financing was arranged with IFC Films, and Sayles made the film in Acapulco for about $1 million.

If you are a newcomer to his work, *Casa de los babys* is likely to be the best Sayles film you have never heard of. The film seems to have less written about it, including fewer interviews, than any other of the director's projects and it earned less than $.5 million in the United States The film has a cast most directors could only dream about: Maggie Gyllenhaal, Daryl Hannah, Marcia Gay Harden, Susan Lynch, Rita Moreno, Mary Steenburgen, and Lili Taylor, plus Vanessa Martinez from *Limbo*. All but Martinez and Moreno play women waiting at the same hotel in an unnamed Latin American country for adoptions to be approved. The hotel, owned by Señora Muñoz (Moreno), is called by the locals "casa de los babys," because of a deal she has worked out with her brother, a lawyer, where he arranges the adoption legalities for women who stay in her hotel. The film deals with the relationships these women form with each other during their stays—which are said to average two months—but it also contrasts the lives these women lead with those of the native population, especially a group of homeless children.

The film is a drama, but it retains the lighter touch that characterized *Sunshine State*. The dialogue that Sayles has written for the six would-be mothers is snappy and often cutting. The premise of the film is reminiscent of *The Women* (George Cukor, 1939), and other films where women were thrown together for extended periods waiting for a divorce in Nevada. It also reminds one of *Secaucus Seven*, though these women had never met before arriving at the hotel. Like many of Sayles's works, this film takes up one of life's milestones, in this case for women who have trouble achieving it in the usual way. Though Sayles usually has focused on life stages defined by age, here chronological age is less important. The women are of different ages, but, with one exception, they are unable to bear children successfully. They also have a variety of other personal difficulties and weaknesses, which make their interactions with each other competitive even though there are no men around for them to fight over.

As one might expect with an ensemble cast of this kind, no one character can be called the film's protagonist, but Nan (Harden) is clearly the chief antagonist. Nan is the personification of the ugly American. She is offensively racist, refuses to speak a word of Spanish, complains constantly about the accommodations, and even steals soap and shampoo from the chambermaid's cart. She has been unable to adopt in the United States because "anger issues" have caused her to be considered unfit, but she thinks of herself as a wonderful mother to her Jack Russell Terriers. The other women discover that she has told them different stories about her background and her husband, though she seems to be from the Midwest. She believes that she is being forced to wait for a child only as a way for the natives to show her who is boss, and she tries to bribe the lawyer to get her baby faster.

The other women at the Casa have different stories and personalities, but none represent Nan's political opposite, which one supposes would be someone with a knowledge of local history and politics, and a sense of the political complications Sayles is exploring in the film (see figure 16). None of the women are there mainly out of altruistic motives, such as those attributed to famous adopters like Madonna and Angelina Jolie. These women are adopting out of self-interest. Leslie (Taylor), a New York editor who is the only one who is physically able to bear a child, wants to adopt so that she doesn't have to deal with the messiness of either a relationship or childbirth. Leslie is the only one who speaks Spanish well, and she also has the sharpest tongue of the group. Her comments about the other women are funny and often dead-on, but also grating, even to those who are not the object of her wit. Skipper (Hanna) from Colorado keeps more to her self than the others, who see her as

Figure 16. Would-be mothers: Eileen (Susan Lynch), Nan (Marcia Gay Harden), Jennifer (Maggie Gyllenhaal), and Skipper (Daryl Hannah).

a fitness freak, but her reserve is explained by the fact that she has lost three babies to a late-term miscarriage and severe birth defects. Jennifer (Gyllenhaal), who lives in Virginia, seems to be hoping that adopting a baby will help hold her marriage together. Her husband is a commodities trader, and she clearly has more money than the others. Eileen (Lynch) is her opposite. A secretary whose husband is currently unemployed, she has to constantly watch her budget, and we see her counting her dwindling currency. She is also not American by birth, having only recently moved to Boston from Ireland. Finally, Gayle (Steenburgen), a Southern born-again Christian and a recovering alcoholic, is the most generous of the women toward her fellow mothers-in-waiting.

The interaction of these women is fascinating, and if the film were a mainstream studio production it would doubtless have accounted for all but a tiny fraction of the story. But this is a Sayles film, so these Americans are put into the context of the ordinary life of the people around them. The film opens not at the Casa, but in the city. We first see the nursery where the babies waiting for adoption are cared for by a loving nurse. We are introduced to three homeless boys as they wake up under crates in an alley and are chased away by an angry shopkeeper. Then we see various shots of workers who live up on the mountain, but whose jobs are mainly in the tourist industry along the shore below. Asunción (Martinez) is shown making breakfast for her siblings and then joining a parade of workers walking to the bus to go down the mountain to work as a maid at the Casa. The bus almost hits the three boys as they run carelessly across the street. Señora Muñoz arrives at her hotel, where she hears of the complaints of the one in 214 (we later learn it is Nan). She also has to tell a very persistent and nice young man, Diómedes (Bruno Bichir), that she has no job for him.

By setting up the narrative in this way, Sayles makes it apparent that the vast disparity in wealth and privilege between most of the natives and the American visitors is a major concern. By showing us a range of local types, we get a picture of the country as itself radically divided between the haves and have-nots, but we also sense that it is not an inherently backward, much less barbaric, place. We get a bit of its political history from Señora Muñoz and her son Buho (Juan Carlos Vives), who is working for her as a handyman now in order to avoid being returned to jail for a charge having something to do with political activity—he's considered "an enemy of the state." He's apparently not very good at his job, because she accuses him of doing more damage with his pliers than he did with Molotov cocktails. He calls the American women fat, corrupt imperialists, while his mother points out that they pay the bills. His father had to go into exile for political reasons, leaving his mother to run the business.

Sayles shows us Buho later out drinking with several of his comrades discussing his mother's adoption business. Why do they need so many, he asks, and his friends respond that Americans are too busy making money to procreate. Buho then argues: "It's just another form of cultural imperialism. We supply the raw material and they refine it. You think they'd let us bring their kids here?" It would be wrong to take Buho as the voice of reason in this film, since he's a dope-smoking ne'er-do-well whose own politics have produced no results. But this question, which is presented as a kind of drunken provocation that produces no response, is nonetheless unsettling. Would Americans be willing to allow foreigners to adopt children born to U.S. citizens? It is hard to imagine that they would, and that difference is a reflection of the power the United States holds over Buho's country. The adopted children will become Americans, learning that culture and not their native one.

Buho told his mother earlier that what she and his uncle Ernesto are doing is selling babies, and his line about "raw material" suggests that the babies have become commodities. His uncle (Pedro Armendáriz) implies that same thing when, at the conclusion of his conversation with Nan, he mutters to himself, "You must forgive us, Madame. But here we do not accept American Express for our children. But there is a cash machine in the lobby." Of course, we know that adoption is a profitable business for him and his sister, but he sees himself as providing a genuine service and upholding the laws of his country. His remarks and Buho's raise larger questions about babies as commodities, not just in this place, but also all over the globe. When added to some of the American women's stories about the medical treatments they went through to try to become pregnant, we have a sense of what a big business the baby market has become.

Despite raising such serious qualms about what these adoptions mean for the cultures of both countries, Sayles's view of them is not reductionist. It is not suggested that the women, even Nan, want babies for illegitimate reasons. They are not depicted as engaging in conspicuous consumption but rather trying to satisfy a deeply felt need. And, Sayles also wants us to see these adoptions as giving the babies a better chance than many would have had in their own country. The story of the homeless boys shows us what might happen to these children if Americans did not want them. Eileen encounters one of them in the market, where she is unaware he has designs on her purse. Ironically, she is the one who could least afford the loss, but she is also shown to be the most generous. She notices the boy before he can make the theft, and buys him a children's book. He seems pleased with the gift, but he can't read and eventually tries unsuccessfully to sell it on the street. The kids manage to earn a bit of money washing windshields, but they use it to buy paint to sniff. We last see them finding a place to sleep under a boat.

The film also shows us from whence the babies the Americans are adopting come. We see Celia (Martha Higareda) for the first time in an interview with a social worker (Lourdes Echevarria), who is talking with her and her mother (Tony Marcin). Celia is 15 and two or three months pregnant. The social worker asks her about having an abortion, but her mother says no to that, and no to the idea of keeping the baby. Celia, when asked what she thinks, looks at her mother and shrugs. This family is clearly not poor, as we see Celia and her mother later shopping and eating in the same upscale restaurant as the would-be mothers from the Casa. Celia approaches the boy we presume to be the father, but cannot or will not tell him about her pregnancy, raising very obliquely the question of male responsibility. But it's not just the middle class that gives up their babies. Asunción too became pregnant when she was fifteen, and she knows that her child is now living in the North. We see her in one scene looking out of a hotel room window at little girls playing in a schoolyard. Tears well up in her eyes. Her pregnancy also meant the end of her schooling, consigning her to the kind of job she now has. What remains unspoken is the lack of birth control in this Catholic country where fifteen-year-olds are commonly sexually active.

Language is another barrier between the Americans and the natives, something which is illustrated brilliantly in a scene between Eileen and Asunción, who has come to make up the room and found Eileen there writing to her relatives in Ireland. Neither character knows much of the other's language, but they have a long conversation. They begin by successfully describing the large families each of them has come from, using their fingers to show numbers. As Asunción makes the bed, Eileen tells in a long monologue the story of a daydream she has had about the daughter she will adopt. It's about a snow day, her child in third grade, and they spend the day together ice-skating. The scene is thus not only presented in a language foreign to the maid, but also what is described must be entirely unfamiliar to this woman from the tropics. Yet, she sits down on the bed, and gives Eileen her full attention, aware from tone and facial expression that something deeply personal is being communicated. Then it's Asunción's turn. She tells of her child up North, who she named Esmeralda, and who she gave her up at the urging of the nuns because she was so young and had to care for her brothers and sisters. She concludes, "I hope my little child has found a mother like you." Eileen, too, knows from the pain in Asunción's face that she has told her something important, but all she can say is, "I didn't get any of it. I'm sorry." Their exchange captures well the imbalance of power and privilege between them. Asunción understands more of what Eileen says because English is the dominant language, but also perhaps because she tries harder. But it may also be better for Eileen that she not understand Asunción's story, since it would make her think about how the mother of her baby would feel.

The film ends with little changed. Diómedes perhaps best represents the limitations of the local economic situation. He still doesn't have a job, his lottery ticket did not come in, and he can't afford to buy the forged passport that would allow him to get into the United States. The other native characters will stay as they are, except perhaps the homeless boys. We wonder whether they will survive to adulthood. Most of the American women will continue as they were as well, but Nan and Eileen, who are perhaps the least and the most deserving, respectively, get their babies. This is not a female version of *Waiting for Godot*, but a realistic study in the global division of wealth and labor, and its impact on some individuals on both sides.

The critics gave *Casa de los babys* a mixed response, more positive than negative, but distinctly less enthusiastic than the one for *Sunshine State*. Stephen Holden's comment in the *New York Times*, "Some of the pieces in its jigsaw puzzle are too fragmentary, and there's a sense of racing against time to fill in the blanks," is typical of the reservations the more positive reviews express. Although the film was reviewed in most of the usual major newspapers and magazines, there seems to have been distinctly less publicity for this film than for any film Sayles had made at least since the 1980s. It is perhaps telling that a reporter for *St. Louis Post-Dispatch* wrote about Sayles calling him up out of the blue to chat about the film (Williams "Call"). In addition, since the title was in Spanish, and about half the dialogue as well, its U.S. audience was limited to those who were willing to read subtitles. Judging by the figures on IMBD, the film did not get wide distribution, so, unfortunately, very few people managed to see one of Sayles's most impressive efforts.

Silver City

Although Sayles has long been identified as a filmmaker concerned with politics in the broad sense of that term, he had largely avoided electoral politics. The closest he had come to examining that subject was in *City of Hope*, where Joe Morton's character, newly elected city councilman, Wynn, is motivated by concerns about future elections and an ambition to higher office. *Silver City* is Sayles's first film to focus on electoral politics. Sayles and producer Maggie Renzi say that the idea for the film emerged out of the stolen 2000 presidential election, especially the disenfranchisement of African American voters in Florida. They are unusually forthright in speaking of the film as an attempt to intervene in the contemporary politics. Renzi says that plans for the film were begun in June 2001, and that they hoped "to make a movie to question where America was going." They felt that many other Americans would "go into a movie theater to think about it, and come out of a movie theater to talk about it" (*Making of Silver City*). The film was shot in September 2003, and opened in the United States a year later. By that time, it may have been too late for this kind of film to have had much impact on the election, even if it had been seen by many voters. This is not a film about George W. Bush or any of the specific criticisms people had leveled at him. Rather, it is a much a broader critique, not only of electoral politics, but also of the general lack of democracy in the United States

Elections have never been the subject of many American films, and the general tenor of those that have been made is somewhat surprising. One might think that Hollywood, especially given the production code's prohibition against demeaning authority, would have presented the American political process in a favorable light, but one would be wrong. The relatively few Hollywood films that have taken up the topic have typically adopted a stance familiar from the behavior and opinions of American voters. In general, these films are cynical about politics and politicians, and some about the social order in the largest sense. The basic assumption is that those in power are all a bunch of crooks—or at least a bunch of careerists whose only interest is self-interest. We might say then that the Sloterdijk/Žižek thesis of more or less conscious disavowal of the truth—"I know all very well but"—is a better account of the way Hollywood's treatment of electoral politics works than the more traditional Marxist one, which holds that the ruling ideas blind people to their own interests.[7] If there is a false consciousness to these films, it lies in the alternative they propose. There is always one exception, the hero of the film, who is incrementally but significantly better—as in *The Candidate* (Michael Ritchie, 1972) or *Bullworth* (Warren Beatty, 1998)—or radically different because he is a complete outsider to politics—as in *Mr. Smith Goes to Washington* (Frank Capra, 1939). The ideology of individualism is doubtless behind this pattern, and I don't believe any of these films assume conscious disavowal of it. But because the ideology of individualism remains unquestioned, Hollywood's treatment of politics can be all the more cynical.

Indeed, one could argue that much of supposed populist Frank Capra's work—including not only *Mr. Smith Goes to Washington*, but also *Meet John Doe* (1941) and *It's a Wonderful Life* (1946)—is even more deeply cynical than most Hollywood films about politics. Capra's films would seem to be performing a kind of critique of ideology, revealing corruption and domination in government, media, and the capitalist order. Yet each of these films offers a patently unreal alternative in the form of a hero who is not only too good to be true but also is either ineffectual or uninterested in change. So in Capra's films, not only is our knowledge of the system's failure disavowed, but also the unreality of the alternative. We know all very well that George Bailey's life is not wonderful, but still we cry when it is restored to him. Capra was widely misinterpreted during his lifetime as offering pro–New Deal parables about the virtues of the common people. We now know that Capra was a lifelong Republican who hated Roosevelt as much as his movie mogul bosses did. This fact helps us to recognize his films as designed to be powerful entertainment rather than lessons in civics.

The cynicism of Hollywood's treatment of politics works at the box office because it seems like common sense. Americans have long been cynical about politics and politicians, which is why so few of us vote. But many who remain cynical about politicians in general make exceptions for those they know well. Polls show that while Americans have low opinions of politicians in general, they typically believe their own elected representatives to be exceptions—which is why incumbents almost always get reelected. This mirrors the one-good-man plot of so many movies. Still, I think even this phenomenon masks a deeper cynicism on the part of voters, who go to the polls in the full awareness that their votes are unlikely to matter. We know very well that all politicians are corrupt, self-serving careerists, but still we go on voting for them because anyone who runs for office must be corrupt and self-serving.

Given the pervasiveness of cynicism about politics, it is perhaps not surprising that *Silver City* would have been perceived as just another instance. As Roger Ebert put it in what was perhaps the most positive review that film received in the mainstream American media, "The movie's strength . . . is not in its outrage, but in its cynicism and resignation." Of course, Ebert isn't using the word "cynicism" in the technical sense, and he thinks that Sayles's cynicism is positive because he doesn't recognize cynicism's dominance. A more perceptive review appeared in *The Observer*, where Philip French remarks that Sayles's recent films "are like Robert Altman movies, but deeper and less cynical." This disagreement between two critics who liked the movie is atypical. The bulk of the reviews of *Silver City*, however, don't see the film as cynical or deep, but rather plodding and obvious. Because the film appeared in the summer before the presidential election and in the wake of Michael Moore's very popular documentary *Fahrenheit 9/11* (2004), many reviewers took the opportunity to point out that *Silver City* would not change anyone's votes, assuming that that must have been the director's goal. Like most of Sayles's films since *Matewan*, critics complain that everything in *Silver City* is black and white.

Although the film leaves no doubt as to which side of the political spectrum the filmmakers are on, it is not a movie that directly addresses the 2004 contest. The film is not about Bush as an individual, but about the way the system works—or fails to work. This is not a fictional *Fahrenheit 9/11*. In *Silver City*, Sayles gives us a critical look at electoral politics without succumbing to cynicism and without offering us the misleading alternative of the good politician. It does not pretend to offer a solution to the problems it identifies, but it does not belittle the attempt to find such solutions either.

Set in the midst of the gubernatorial campaign of political scion Dickie Pilager (Chris Cooper), our protagonist is Danny O'Brien (Danny Huston, son of *Maltese Falcon* director, John Huston), a former investigative journalist now working as an investigator for a private detective agency. He is hired by Pilager campaign manger, the Karl Rove–ish Chuck Raven (Richard Dreyfuss), to find out who might have planted a corpse in the lake where a Pilager environmental spot was being shot. Danny discovers that the corpse is not the result of a malicious prank but something more like the return of the repressed. The dead man turns out to be an undocumented worker who died because of poor safety practices at a meatpacking plant, and who was buried at an abandoned mine site to keep the accident a secret. The mine site was once owned by Dickie Pilager, but it has since been purchased from him for more than it was worth by Wes Benteen (Kris Kristofferson) and is now slated to become Silver City, an upscale resort development. The site is an environmental nightmare, full of toxic metals and honeycombed with mineshafts, some now filled with water under such pressure that it forced the buried worker out of the ground and into a stream that carried him to the lake. Danny is able to uncover the truth about the death, but to no end. The authorities are uninterested in challenging anyone with influence and allow the death of the worker to be blamed on a low-level thug.

Silver City marks Sayles's return to remaking a standard Hollywood genre, which he had last done in *Lone Star*, but here the genre remains closer to the surface. The genre in question is the hard-boiled detective story, and Sayles mentions Raymond Chandler as an inspiration, because his work getting the solution to the mystery is almost as interesting as the solution. And he observes that Philip Marlowe, as he is trying to solve the mystery, "takes you places in Los Angeles in that period that you ordinarily wouldn't go." This connection is apt, because in Chandler's novels, the detective learns of economic and social inequalities, but is powerless to change them. Marlowe is heroic not because he can establish justice, but because he believes it matters. But Chandler's view is limited to a very general picture of the corruption of those in power and the class that controls them. *Silver City* gives us a much more precise lesson about who holds the power in society and how they corrupt the electoral system to maintain that power.

Sayles thinks of Chandler's Marlowe as the sort of "guide" that appears in different guises in many of the director's films, and Danny is another such figure. The viewer, like Danny, learns how the system works as the murder is investigated. That's not to say that the lessons taught are doctrinaire, or that they are, as is sometimes suggested, full of easy solutions. *Silver City* does not offer a solution. The most important thing that Danny learns is something the knightly Marlowe never had to: that his efforts matter despite the outcome. When we first meet Danny, he tells his former editor and current Web journalist, Mitch (Tim Roth), that he doesn't do politics anymore because its bad for his mental health, and there's "nothing I can do about it, anyway." Mitch, when he finds out what case Danny is working on, accuses him of having gone over to the other side. Danny's discovery of the truth behind the Pilager campaign leads him to believe again that he can do something. The biggest lesson of *Silver City* lies not in the details of corruption and self-interest, but in the very effort that Danny makes despite his self-interest.

In the broad outline of its plot, *Silver City* sticks very close to the traditional formula for the hard-boiled detective story. A body is discovered, a detective is hired, and he begins to investigate. After some efforts, the detective loses his original client but continues to work on his own. In Danny's case, he is fired because Chuck Raven finds out he used to be a journalist. As in the classic form of Chandler's original Marlowe novels, Danny is successful at solving the mystery, but not in changing the larger corrupt social order that produced the crime. However, Danny differs from Marlowe in several significant ways. In the first place, he is an employee, not a small-business owner. This makes him more vulnerable but it also makes his own interests less dependent on those of the client. He is labor, not management. Secondly, his character is less like Philip Marlowe, than Jake Gittes. Like Jack Nicholson's character in *Chinatown* (Roman Polanski, 1974), Danny is not very good at his job, though in ways that distinguish him from Gittes. He is apparently congenitally indiscreet, is not in the least intimidating, and is easily seduced by Maddy Pilager (Daryl Hannah), the candidate's estranged sister and one of the people he's been told to investigate. Moreover, Danny Huston is not Jack Nicholson, and putting a nonstar in this kind of role makes all the difference. Jake Gittes may fail, but he fails glamorously, having Jack Nicholson's charisma, a great wardrobe, and Faye Dunaway to boot. Danny's failure is ordinary failure. He's not handsome, dresses badly, and spends the entire picture depressed over two girlfriends who have walked out on him. He seems to be what several people call him, a loser, and yet he is willing to risk his neck and his job for the sake of the truth. He is, in other words, a more realistic version of the detective hero.

Dickie Pilager is if anything more inept than Danny—he is certainly much less intelligent—yet because of his birth into a wealthy and powerful family, he is a winner. Like George W. Bush, Dickie can't utter a complete sentence. Those around him including his father, Judson Pilager (Michael Murphy) a U.S. Senator, know he's not very bright. But if he's bumbling and inarticulate, he is not evil. Mitch says that there is not a corrupt bone in his body, and that he's a true believer. His last name may have once accurately characterized the family, but applied to him it is ironic, since it's impossible to imagine this guy pillaging anything. Chris Cooper plays him as slow but gentle, and you develop a certain sympathy for him as a kind of victim of those who have more brains but no scruples.

The real pillager is located outside of politics proper in the figure of the oligarch Benteen. He is the kind of power behind the thrown we saw represented by Alan King's Murray in *Sunshine State*, but he is much more evil because he is much more powerful. Early on in the film, we are shown a chart that makes Benteen's holdings look like an octopus, with tentacles reaching into every part of the economy. He is the chief financial backer of the Pilagers' campaigns, but their businesses are also interconnected. The Pilagers got rich off a gold mine Dickie's grandfather got title to as payment for dry goods. They have long since diversified and now own a business with Benteen that cleans up "cow pies," many of which are produced by the cattle one of Benteen's other firms raises. The metaphor goes by so quickly that you may not get it the first time.

Dickie Pilager is represented throughout the film as mouthing slogans and sound bites designed either to resonate with the conservative faithful who have supported his father, or to be so bland as to not offend anyone else. The environmental spot the film opens with is a perfect example of the latter, as are the titles interspersed between some scenes that tell us things like "Richard Pilager cares about the Family," and culminating with "Richard Pilager cares about *YOU*." These are the lies, half-truths, and irrelevancies candidates tell us in order to get elected. For the truth, we need to hear from Benteen.

In one of the film's most effective scenes, Benteen and Dickie are horseback riding, and the oligarch gives the candidate an ideology lesson (see figure 17). Here as in *Matewan*, one character is teaching another but teaching the audience as well. Benteen asks Dickie what he sees as they ride through a pristine Western landscape, and the candidate answers, tentatively, like a student who is worried he may not know what the teacher wants, "Mountains." Benteen replies, "I see a big sign that says, 'No Americans allowed.'" He compares government controlled or regulated lands in the West to "a treasure chest waiting to be opened. Only there's a 500 pound bureaucrat sitting on it." When Dickie starts to talk about the people, Benteen says that they need to be led by the horns to know what's good for them and that only those who see the big picture end up with "the shiny stuff." After Benteen

Figure 17. Wes Benteen (Kris Kristofferson) gives Dickie Pilager (Chris Cooper) an ideology lesson.

tells the candidate that in two weeks he will have to call him governor, we get the following exchange:

> BENTEEN: You know what the big picture is, don't you Dickie?
> DICKIE: (looking puzzled) um, it's a . . .
> BENTEEN: Privatization. The land was meant for the citizens, not them damn pencil pushers in Washington.
> DICKIE: Like this Silver City deal?
> BENTEEN: That's just a pile of mine debris I'm trying to unload. Son, we got resources here you wouldn't believe, untapped resources. You and your dad are the point men in a fight to liberate those resources for the American people.

The scene may seem simply to tell us something we all already know, that the rich own the politicians. But it does more than that. It illustrates how the language of populism is used by the few to justify their interests and sustain their hegemony. It thus offers a critique of ideology, neatly exemplifying one of Marx's and Engels's definitions of the term, as a thought process where "men and their circumstances appear upside down as in a camera obscura" (47).

Silver City makes it clear that individual politicians are not the roots of the problem, and that individual heroes are not going to solve it. Opposing the powerful is left to a solo investigator and some bloggers, and the film shows that, while they may learn the truth, they cannot prevail as individuals. But this dark vision of electoral politics is not cynical because it goes beyond the common place that "they are all a bunch of crooks." Sayles asks us to look at the system with fresh eyes and suggests that only radical change will remedy its defects. Moreover, the film is not entirely pessimistic, avoiding the sense of inevitable failure that the end of *Chinatown* conveys. Danny has left a road map to the connections he's uncovered with Mitch's online magazine, and he has paid out of his own pocket to return the dead man's body to his family in Mexico. In our last glimpse of Danny, he is walking away with his arms around Nora (Maria Bello), one of the girl friends who had dumped him. She has called off her wedding to lobbyist Chandler (Billy Zane) after she complained about Benteen buying the newspaper for which she reports. He looks less like a loser here than at any time in the picture.

The sale of Nora's paper to Benteen points to one of two important themes in *Silver City* not yet discussed, the decline and increasing monopolization of the media. Danny, Mitch, and Nora, were all journalists, and all are shown to have had their investigative work curtailed by the power of corporations and by the degradation of traditional news media into pure "entertainment." Nora's newspaper has already undergone a buyout causing the news staff to be reduced, but now they will be owned by the very guy they should be keeping tabs on most. Mitch's alternative publication was forced to abjure politics after an investigative piece Danny wrote turned out to be wrong, a set-up that successfully intimidated the owners into firing them. Mitch's current Web-based project seems to be the hope that's left for journalism, something Sayles might not have been as likely to suggest had the film been made a few years later after the Right seems to have made better use of that medium as well.

The other issue that Sayles highlights is the hypocrisy surrounding undocumented workers. Such workers are shown to be fundamental to industries such as construction, agriculture, and meatpacking, where they are allowed to work if their employers are powerful enough. The victim whose body turns up at the beginning of the film was killed in an accident at a slaughterhouse, where proper safety procedures had not been followed and where regulation was lax because of Benteen's political influence. The worker was brought to this country by a contractor who is said to keep his workers in debt to him, in effect making them indentured servants. These workers are used because they are so easily exploited, having no recourse to government protections because they are illegal. What is unspoken in the film is that the Right blames the workers for coming here, but not the employers who exploit them.

Silver City contrasts its own investigation into the reality of American politics with the commercials produced for the Pilager campaign that distort that reality. We see two of these being made, at the beginning and end of the film. In each case, we see a glossy surface created, which is not so much false as distracting. This may seem to be a version of the postmodern critique, which says that today the surface and the simulacra are all that we have left to us. Sayles's point, however, is exactly the opposite. We can learn to see through the lies and to recognize the distractions, and it's his job to help us do this. Moreover, each commercial is interrupted by a reality that refuses to remain hidden. In the opening spot, Dickie snags the body, which literally would not stay buried. The concluding commercial features a chorus singing "America the Beautiful" as the candidate addresses us in front of the same beautiful lake. This time, dead fish begin to appear on the surface, and, as the film ends, we see their floating bodies litter the lake from shore to shore.

Sayles's film is a thoughtful and entertaining look at contemporary American politics, but it may also be his most underestimated work. The critics liked this film less well than *Sunshine State* or *Casa de los babys*, though it did not produce the degree of hostile response generated by *Limbo*. The mixed reviews suggest that many critics didn't get what Sayles was attempting to do. That seems to be the case with the audience as well, who mainly stayed away. The film got somewhat wider distribution than his previous one, but it still grossed just $1 million. Some of this is doubtless the result of the film being distributed by Newmarket Films, a small independent company that had a surprise hit with *Memento* (Christopher Nolan, 2000), a film it produced. By 2004, the independent film sector was shrinking rapidly, and Sayles's ability to get his films into theaters was significantly impacted.

Honeydripper

Honeydripper, the sixteenth film by John Sayles, opened in New York and Los Angeles in late December 2007. The film centers around the Honeydripper Lounge, a rural Alabama night club in 1950, whose owner, Tyrone (Pine Top) Purvis (Danny Glover), is trying to save his failing business by bringing in a famous electric-guitar player for a one-night stand. Shot on location, the film cost an estimated $5 million to make, a substantial portion of which the director himself invested from the proceeds of screenwriting for hire. Sayles was unable to secure financing or a distribution deal even with a company like Newmarket. U.S. theatrical distribution was handled by Emerging Pictures, a small company run by Ira Deutchman who had previously been involved in founding both Cinecom and Fine Line Features. Because of a lack of funds for traditional promotion, innovative alternatives were tried. Sayles promoted the film personally by traveling to festivals and college campuses, and efforts were made to reach African American college students, especially at historically black institutions. Another marketing ploy involved sending musicians from the film, billed as the Honeydripper All-Star Band, to blues festivals. With the campus screenings and other nontraditional venues, it's hard to know how large an audience the film finally reached. According to IMBD, the film never played on more than nineteen screens at one time.

In trying to get *Honeydripper* into theaters Sayles was struggling with changes in the independent film market. As the cost of producing high-quality images continued to decline, more and more films were being made. At the same time, most of the major studios were closing or absorbing their "classics" or other divisions that had financed or distributed independent films. The average cost of Hollywood films continued to increase, and even films that continued to be supported by Miramax or Focus Features were likely to cost at least $25 million.

Honeydripper is the most traditionally structured film Sayles has made, at least since *The Brother from Another Planet*. There are three distinct acts, and the third one presents a clear resolution to the conflict set up in the first. The plot is a reworking of one the oldest stories in Hollywood, in which a musical or dramatic performance is the last hope to save a promoter, a theater, or a club from ruin. Versions of it came in with the sound era, and were repeated regularly at least through the 1950s. A culinary rendering of it was *Big Night* (Campbell Scott, Stanley Tucci, 1996). Like that film, what *Honeydripper* does with the familiar story makes all the difference. It is set in a convincingly authentic recreation of the Jim Crow South, focusing on African Americans. Tyrone is a piano player who grew up with jazz and toured nationally during the swing era. He runs the Honeydripper with the help of Maceo (Charles Dutton). His top act has been Bertha Mae (Mable John), a blues singer in the style of Bessie Smith or Ma Rainey, whom Tyrone accompanies on the piano. Tyrone loves this music, but the juke joint next door is getting all the customers because its box has all the latest records. Tyrone is behind on the rent for his club, and his landlord is threatening to evict him. The Sheriff (Stacy Keach) comes by to make vague threats; he is a "partner" of most black business owners in his county, and he doesn't like it that Tyrone has so far managed to stay afloat without his patronage. To try to save his club, Tyrone books Guitar Sam, a rising star on radio and records, who plays the new-style rhythm and blues and will bring in young people. In the meantime, Sonny (Gary Clark Jr.) a young man just out of the army gets off the freight train he was riding in Harmony, and Tyrone offers him a meal. He leaves his bags at the club and goes off to look for work. He is picked up by the Sheriff for "vagrancy" and forced to harvest cotton to "work of his debt to society" and fatten the county coffers. When Guitar Sam fails to show, Tyrone discovers the electric guitar Sonny has left with him and persuades the Sheriff to let Sonny out of jail for the weekend so that he can impersonate the missing musician. Because they don't believe Sonny can play, the plan is to fake a power failure just as Sonny begins his act. When the big night arrives, the club is full of soldiers and farmhands, and Sonny, dressed in gaudy new clothes quickly sewn for the occasion, is a smashing success, able to carry off the impersonation musically and charismatically. The club is saved, but the Sheriff winds up as Tyrone's partner, having used his influence to keep the club in Tyrone's hands after the landlord threatens to evict him even after the rent is paid.

While *Honeydripper* hews far more closely to a single main plotline than most of Sayles's films, there are some important and engaging subplots. Bertha Mae dies during the night after we saw her performing in the Honeydripper. She leaves a companion, Slick (Vondie Curtis-Hall), who had been her driver and then her manager. Tyrone and Delilah arrive at Bertha Mae's house hoping to borrow some money to save the club, only to discover that not only has she passed away, but that she had no money left when she died. Later, there is a funeral procession and burial in which the coffin is carried from the church to cemetery by the pallbearers. Delilah works part time as a housekeeper for Amanda (Mary Steenburgen), a woman who grew up dirt poor but who married into one of most prominent families in Harmony. There is just one extended scene between these two characters, but it reveals another aspect of race relations in the period, the intimacy between white employers and their black servants. In that scene, Delilah tells how she and Tyrone met and what he has meant to her. She has been attending a tent revival, hoping that the Spirit will move her to come forward to be saved. But she can't get passed the condemnation of her husband that is at least implicit in the preacher's rhetoric, because she knows that he is a good man. She finally decides to leave the tent and go to the Honeydripper to help her husband on his big night.

Realism is the dominant aesthetic in *Honeydripper*, but it does have one magical-realist element, the character of Possum, played by bluesman Keb' Mo.' Possum is a blind guitar player who is most often seen sitting and playing in the center of Harmony. But he is only seen by other musicians. When we are first introduced to him, the camera follows Sonny down a sidewalk and then pans around to show Possum in a place that had been empty a second earlier. Like the Mother in *Men with Guns*, Possum seems to know the future, but also like her, his foreknowledge does no one any good. Possum's literal invisibility to most people might be read as a metaphor for the figurative invisibility of most African Americans. He also represents, in the kind of music he plays, both the past and the future, the tradition of blues guitar that Tyrone would have regarded as primitive and the triumph of that style when transformed into rock & roll.

Honeydripper is about race relations under Jim Crow, but it is a subtle, nuanced treatment of the topic. There are no lynchings or other examples of the worst excesses of racism during the period. The Sheriff is a petty tyrant, but he is not a killer like Charlie Wade was in *Lone Star*. He doesn't seem to hate black people, but he assumes it is his right to dominate them. There is a very clear set of rules that blacks have learned and whites expect to be obeyed. To illustrate, in the scene in which Sonny is picked up by the Sheriff, the first thing the lawman demands is that he take his hat off, and Sonny apologizes for not having done it without being asked. It was something that white men expected black men to do. Then when Sonny tells the Sheriff that he is looking for work, he is pressed into involuntary servitude, a practice common during cotton harvest. The Sheriff sells Sonny's labor to a plantation owner who pays the county rather than Sonny. But if these incidents make clear the injustice of the segregated South, the film does not dwell on them, perhaps because to do so would have made whites much more central to the story.

Rather, the movie shows how African Americans found ways to maintain themselves and their dignity despite being defined by those in power as second-class citizens. Tyrone understands the rules by which he must operate, but he has managed to build his own business that involves music, something that he loves. He has survived a violent and dissolute past to become a loving husband to Delilah (Lisa Gay Hamilton) and stepfather to China Doll (Yaya DaCosta). He has spent his life in music playing piano, and he can't understand the rising tide of the guitar. Yet, he is willing to take a chance, and in the end, he embraces the new music, showing both his general ability to adapt and survive and his openness to artistic innovation.

The year 1950 is a moment on the cusp of many important political and cultural developments. We don't associate it with either the Civil Rights Movement or the emergence of rock and roll, but both were already in progress even if they weren't recognized as such. In 1950 the Korean War was beginning, and President Truman had only recently ordered that the armed forces be fully integrated, probably the most significant step toward racial equality since the Fifteenth Amendment. The struggle against inequality did not begin with Rosa Parks or lunch-counter sit-ins; it had been going on since reconstruction. In 1950, for example, various legal challenges to Jim Crow were being made, and one that was filed in 1951, Brown v. Board of Education, would eventually be settled by the Supreme Court in 1954, perhaps the key moment for the movement against segregation that would develop strength throughout the decade. Sayles refers to the integration of the military, and there is a scene of a newly reopened, integrated army base. But what *Honeydripper* demonstrates is the strength of character that underlies this nearly century-long struggle.

Most of all, however, *Honeydripper* is about the music. Although this is his first film to focus on music, Sayles has always taken a deep interest in the music for his films. His collaboration with Mason Daring, who has composed music for every one of his films except *Baby, It's You*, has been more important than any other except with producer Renzi. For this film, Sayles cowrote four songs, including "China Doll," one of the numbers Sonny performs. Most of the music performed in the film was actually played on camera (see figure 18). Gary Clark Jr. was chosen for his role, his first, because he was an up-and-coming blues artist. His acting is as quiet and reserved as his playing is brash and expressive. His musical performance is authentic and energizing.

Sayles is as interested in music history as he is in social history. The figure of Guitar Sam is based on Guitar Slim, born Eddie Jones, a Mississippi blues guitarist who made a name for himself in New Orleans for his flamboyant style of dress and performance. During a national

Figure 18. Sonny (Gary Clark Jr.) rocks the Honeydripper Lounge as Guitar Sam.

tour, Guitar Slim was involved in an auto accident, and other performers played in his stead but under his name. In the early 1950s, before television and the movies had picked up on rock and roll, most listeners would not know what performers looked like, so this charade could be pretty safely carried off. Sayles describes the musical era of the film as a very brief one between swing and rock and roll, which featured the jump blues of Louis Jordan, and other forms of rhythm and blues that would mutate into rock and roll in a few years (DVD commentary). This music has not often turned up in its original form in movies, though Carl Franklin used recordings from this moment very effectively to create period feel and mood in *Devil in a Blue Dress* (1995). By putting the music in the foreground, Sayles shows us where rock and roll came from, both musically, in a transformation where the electric guitar replaced both the piano and saxophone to become the dominant instrument in popular music, and culturally, before it became the music of white teenagers. The first song Sonny plays as Guitar Sam is "Good Rockin' Tonight," a composition of Roy Brown he recorded in 1948 that is always mentioned as one of candidates for the first rock and roll song. Wynonie Harris would have a hit with it in the early 1950s that Elvis Presley heard and then covered for Sam Phillips's Sun Records.

Honeydripper is an astonishingly well-made realist drama. The cast is superb, and, as usual, Sayles gets great performances from them. The cinematographer was Dick Pope, whose credits include many of Mike Leigh's films and Neil Burger's *The Illusionist* (2006), for which he received an Oscar nomination. His images have a warmth and luminosity that lends these more or less humble locations a distinct but believable beauty. The screenplay builds to an effective and pleasing resolution, and the characters are invariably well drawn. All of these qualities, in addition to its subject matter, make this a film, as Renzi has said, "for adults" (DVD commentary). *Honeydripper* strikes one as an old-fashioned movie in the best sense. There's even a little bit of the old dream factory here, with Sonny turning out to be good enough to save the Honeydripper Lounge. It is, therefore, even more than most of Sayles's films, not what one expects these days to find in whatever it is that passes for an art house. But perhaps more important, it is not what people expect of cinema today when the popular films are made for teenage boys. While that has been true for many years, the number of films that are not made for this audience seems to be smaller every year. It may be that narrative, which in the studio era was the dominant characteristic of film, has now become simply a way to stage a spectacle, a new cinema of attractions.

While *Honeydripper* received generally favorable reviews, doing better with the critics than either *Silver City* or *Casa de los babys*, the notices seem more respectful than enthusiastic. It was also reviewed in fewer periodicals than these films, with *Time*, *Newsweek*, and *Rolling Stone* (of all places) ignoring it. A number of critics applauded Sayles for making a less dour or pessimistic film, and the acting and story were generally praised. Many critics recognized the quality of the film, but few were able to make it seem as though their readers needed to see it. The more negative reviews were perhaps more instructive. Most of them complained about what they perceived to be the film's slow pacing, which is understandable if your reference point is the average pace of contemporary studio productions. What I think is most striking about these notices is not their explicit judgments, but the sense, which many of them convey, that Sayles isn't very interesting to the critics anymore. Given the distribution difficulties and the lack of a critical groundswell, it is not surprising that *Honeydripper* grossed less than $300,000.

In the wake of his experience with *Honeydripper* there were rumors that John Sayles had directed his last film. It was said that although he could find money to make films, it had become impossible to get them distributed. The rumors said that he would continue to write screenplays, both for hire and on spec. But in 2010, Sayles had finished a new film, *Amigo*, about the Philippine-American War of the early twentieth century. Shot in the Philippines with a local crew and mostly local cast, Sayles and Renzi made the movie for an estimated cost of just above $1 million. The script is based on a part of Sayles's novel, *A Moment in the Sun*, for which he has had difficulty finding a publisher.[8] *Amigo* premiered at Cinemalaya, the Philippine Independent Film Festival in July 2010 and had its North American opening at the Toronto International Film Festival in September of that year. It was screened at film festivals around the world as Sayles and Renzi tried to find a distributor. It has recently been announced that the film would be released by Variance Films on August 20, 2011.

Notes

1. On the genre of the relationship story, see Shumway, 157–87.

2. For reviews from lesbian perspectives, see Rizzo, Marney, and DiCaprio. For scholarly criticism, see Gaines, Stacey, Straayer, and Merck.

3. For an analysis of the various states of alienation in *Brother*, see Subramanian.

4. Foner's view of *Matewan* is on the whole much more positive, but he too complains about a lack of broader historical and political context (206). He also notes that Sayles does not refer to Mother Jones, "one of West Virginia's most celebrated union organizers," depicting "the working class as by definition male." But as Foner himself acknowledges, this was a period when most "women occupied subordinate places in cohesive, family-oriented communities." On issues like this, Foner seems to put Sayles in the position of having to be historically inaccurate so that the film would be more relevant to a world where "more Americans work at McDonald's restaurants or as secretaries than in steel mills or coal mines" (207), and where women's subordination is perhaps a more important issue than class.

5. Limón reads *Lone Star* in terms of the same allegory, but with opposite interpretation, arguing that unlike in *High Noon*, where Will Kane (Gary Cooper) has left his Latina lover to marry an Anglo, Pilar and Sam's bond implies an ending of the colonial order (242).

6. Handley refers to Irwin in support of his reading *Lone Star* as an Oedipal allegory about the nation (162).

7. Sloterdijk's *Critique of Cynical Reason* is the source of the conception of cynicism as "enlightened false consciousness," but Žižek's formulation, "I know all very well but . . ." has reached a much wider audience.

8. *A Moment in the Sun* was published May 17, 2011, by McSweeneys of San Francisco.

Interviews with John Sayles

Because Sayles has sat for so many interviews, in lieu of a single one, the following is a bibliography of key interviews given by the director throughout his career, followed by a sampling of comments from these materials. Readers should also consult Diane Carson, ed., *John Sayles: Interviews*. Jackson: University of Mississippi Press, 1999.

Chute, David. "John Sayles: Designated Writer." *Film Comment* 17 (May/June 1981): 54–59. Reprinted in Carson, *John Sayles*, 3–14.

An early interview that deals with the beginnings of his career and the making of *The Return of the Secaucus Seven.*

Dreifus, Claudia. "John Sayles." *The Progressive* 55 (Nov. 1991): 30–33. Reprinted in Carson, *John Sayles*, 136–44.

A wide-ranging interview about Sayles's career through *City of Hope,* especially interesting for comments about the relationship of his films to those of other directors.

Foner, Eric. "A Conversation between Eric Foner and John Sayles." *Past Imperfect: History according to the Movies*, ed. Mark C. Cairns. New York: Holt, 1996.

An interview conducted by an eminent American historian that focuses on Sayles's views of history and films about it.

Georgakas, Dan. "Don't Make Your Dreams Too Small: An Interview with John Sayles." *Cineaste* 33.2 (2008): 2, 14–19.

Career reflections, the current state of independent cinema, and *Honeydripper.*

Kemp, Philip. "Sweet Home Alabama." *Sight and Sound* 18.6 (2008): 12.

About music in *Honeydripper.*

The Making of Silver City. Video. Dir. and prod., Donnie L. Betts. *Silver City*. DVD. Culver City, Calif.: Columbia Tristar Home Entertainment, 2004.

Unusually explicit and revealing comments about Sayles's and Renzi's motives for making *Silver City* and about their political views.

Mitchell, Sean. "Bard of the Low Budget." *Los Angeles Times*, Oct. 20, 1991. http://articles.latimes.com/1991–10–20/entertainment/ca-90_1_john-sayles; accessed Sept. 20, 2011.

Revealing comments about financing, distribution, and the problems of finding an audience.

Neff, Gina. "Reel to Real History: A Conversation with John Sayles and Howard Zinn." *Radical Society* 29 (July 2002): 25–38.

A conversation about history, especially American history, which reveals Sayles's deep interest and knowledge of it.

O'Sullivan, Eleanor. "Director's Humanism Keeps Him Away from Mainstream Movies." *Asbury Park Press*, Aug. 23, 1987.

Some of Sayles's most explicit statements about the politics of film, and of his own films. Reprinted in Carson, *John Sayles,* 86–89.

Rauzi, Robin. "The Indie Icon." *Los Angeles Times*, Mar. 1, 1998, 7.

Making *Men with Guns,* the importance of setting, and the growth of the independent film sector.

Sicha, Choire. "An Indie Line in the Sand." *Los Angeles Times*, Dec. 23, 2007, E.3.

An interview with both Maggie Renzi and Sayles on the distribution and promotion of *Honeydripper*.

Smith, Gavin, ed., and John Sayles. *Sayles on Sayles*. London: Faber and Faber, 1998.

A trove of information and ideas about Sayles's career from the Roger Corman days through *Men with Guns.*

Stein, Harry. "How John Sayles Learned to Stop Worrying and Love the Studio." *Premiere* (July 1999): 90–110.

An enlightening discussion of Sayles's relationship to the industry.

West, Joan W., and Dennis West. "Not Playing By the Usual Rules: An Interview with John Sayles." *Cineaste* (Sept. 1999): 28–31.

Detailed and engaging discussion of *Limbo.*

———. "John Sayles: Borders and Boundaries." *The Cineaste Interviews 2,*

ed. Gary Crowdus and Dan Georgakas. Chicago: Lake View, 2002 [1996]. Reprinted in Carson, *John Sayles*, 210–18.
A focus on the ideas that have interested scholars most in *Lone Star*.

Sayles has also provided detailed audio commentary on the following films on DVD:

Return of the Secaucus Seven. Restored Version. UCLA Film and Television Archive, Anarchists Convention, Inc. and IFC Films. Los Angeles: MGM Home Entertainment, 2003.
Lianna. Restored Version. UCLA Film and Television Archive, Anarchists Convention, Inc. and IFC Films. Los Angeles: MGM Home Entertainment, 2003.
The Secret of Roan Inish. Skerry Movies Corporation. Culver City, Calif.: Sony Pictures Home Entertainment, 2007.
Men with Guns. Anarchist's Convention Films and Independent Film Channel. Culver City, Calif.: Columbia TriStar Home Entertainment, 2003.
Limbo. Screen Gems. Culver City, Calif.: Columbia TriStar Home Entertainment, 1999.
Sunshine State. Sony Pictures Classics. Culver City, Calif.: Columbia TriStar Home Entertainment, 2001.
Casa de los babys. Casa Productions and IFC Films. Los Angeles: MGM Home Entertainment, 2004.
Honeydripper. Honeydripper Films. New York: Screen Media Films, 2008.

Excerpts

ON THE POLITICS OF ENTERTAINMENT:

"But people forget that entertainment for entertainment's sake has a political message too. . . . It may not be an overt one but it's certainly there and it's an easy one to accept: 'This is kind of a nice world, a nice way to think about ourselves.' Other realities are for other people and they deserve those realities, is the message. If those other people are having a hard time then there's probably something wrong with them, the message says. But there's nothing wrong with you or the system that makes your good life possible, so you don't have to worry about it too much." (O'Sullivan in Carson, *Interviews* 87)

ON GENRE:

"I'm a writer. I write stuff and then I realize, 'This doesn't really fit into any genre.' Usually, when I have to pitch a script to a potential backer, I have to tell the story. I find I can't say, 'This is a cross between *Rambo* and *Missing*.' My pieces tend to be in between genres. They tend to be about characters, about situations, rather than, say, 'an action-adventure-police story.'" (Dreifus 30)

ON CHOOSING TITLES AND FINDING AN AUDIENCE FOR HIS FILMS:

"I'm very bad at titles. *Matewan* is not a great-selling title, but I never thought of anything better," he says as we walk the streets of Hoboken on the way to a restaurant. "So that's what we stayed with. Our joke about *City of Hope* is that the working title was *Sex, Lies and Urban Renewal*. One of the problems that we have is that we're asking more from moviegoers than most movies ask. We're asking for them to pay attention for the whole movie. You know, I liked *Terminator 2* fine, for what it was, but you can leave the theater and come back five minutes later, and you're not lost. You know that the guy is still running after him. It's like a *Roadrunner* cartoon. But in our movies, if you miss five minutes, you're lost." (Mitchell)

ON THE BUSH ADMINISTRATION AND *SILVER CITY*:

"Right now, I feel like the people that are running the American government are there to destroy it except for the military. That their ideology is there should be less government. There should be fewer services. People should get used to having fewer services. That that was a mistake to start those things like social security, and public education, and public health works . . . in the first place. And that if they can get us into enough wars and run up a big enough debt and cut taxes at the same time, they will have an excuse to tell the people, 'look, there's no way we will have enough to give you those services, so you are going to have to go along with them.' And then people will get used to not having them, and people will totally change their idea of what government should be. . . . With *Silver City*, I think a lot of what I would like people to think about as they see the movie is that there is cause and effect in the world. There are things that happen by accident, but there a lot of things that don't happen by accident. Once you know that people are doing them, especially your own government, or people that you have allowed to run your own government, there is something you can do about it." (*The Making of Silver City*)

ON WHY HE ATTEMPTS TO IMMERSE VIEWERS IN A PLACE:

"You really try to choose your locations so they're telling a story. That's why we shot [*Men with Guns*] all over Mexico instead of one little area. If I had more money I probably would have shot in four different countries. Then, I have a philosophy of writing where I do as much research as I can. First reading research, but usually also a trip to the place to talk to the people. Then in preproduction, we'll show the script to the people we're going to be working with, the people who are going to be in it and who it's about. And we say, does this seem right? And the final thing we do is we try to cast as many of the small parts as we can locally. So in *Lone Star*, we probably had twenty-five actors from Texas." (Rauzi)

Filmography

Return of the Secaucus Seven (1980)
Production Company: Salsipuedes Productions
Distributor: Libra/Specialty
Producers: William Aydelott, Jeffrey Nelson
Unit Manager: Maggie Renzi
Director: John Sayles
Screenplay: John Sayles
Cinematography: Austin de Besche
Editor: John Sayles
Music: Mason Daring
Songs: Adam LeFevre
Sound: Wayne Wadhams
Cast: Bruce MacDonald (Mike Donnelly), Katie Sipriano (Maggie Renzi), Adam LeFevre (J.T.), Maggie Cousineau (Frances Carlson), Gordon Clapp (Chip Hollister), Jean Passanante (Irene Rosenblue), Karen Trott (Maura Tolliver), Mark Arnott (Jeff Andrews), David Strathairn (Ron Desjardins), John Sayles (Howie)
Format: 16 mm (1.37 : 1)
104 min.

Lianna (1983)
Production Company: Winwood Productions
Distributor: United Artists Classics
Producers: Jeffrey Nelson, Maggie Renzi
Director: John Sayles
Screenplay: John Sayles
Cinematography: Austin De Besche
Editor: John Sayles
Music: Mason Daring
Art Direction: Jeanne McDonnell
Cast: Linda Griffiths (Lianna), Jane Hallaren (Ruth), Jon DeVries (Dick), Jo Henderson (Sandy), Jessica MacDonald (Theda), Jesse Solomon (Spencer),

John Sayles (Bob), Stephen Mendillo (Bob), Betsy Julia Robinson (Cindy), Nancy Mette (Kim), Maggie Renzi (Sheila)
Format: 16 mm (1.78 : 1)
110 min.

Baby It's You (1983)
Production Companies: Double Play Productions, Paramount Pictures
Distributor: Paramount Pictures
Producers: Griffin Dunne, Amy Robinson
Associate Producer: Robert F. Colesberry
Director: John Sayles
Screenplay: John Sayles
Story: Amy Robinson
Cinematography: Michael Ballhaus
Editor: Sonya Polonsky
Music: Joel Dorn
Recorded Music Performers: The Shirelles, Sam the Sham and the Pharaohs, Bruce Springsteen, Dusty Springfield, The Trashmen, The Supremes, The Righteous Brothers, Frank Sinatra, Procol Harum
Production Design: Jeffrey Townsend
Cast: Rosanna Arquette (Jill Rosen), Vincent Spano (Albert "Sheik" Capadilupo), Joanna Merlin (Mrs. Rosen), Jack Davidson (Dr. Rosen), Nick Ferrari (Mr. Capadilupo), Dolores Messina (Mrs. Capadilupo), Leora Dana (Miss Vernon), Bill Raymond (Mr. Ripeppi), Sam McMurray (Mr. McManus), Liane Curtis (Jody), Claudia Sherman (Beth), Marta Kober (Debra), Tracy Pollan (Leslie), Frank Vincent (Vinnie), Matthew Modine (Steve), Robert Downey Jr. (Stewart)
Format: 35 mm (1.78 : 1)
105 min.

The Brother from Another Planet (1984)
Production Company: A-Train Films
Distributor: Cinecom Pictures
Producers: Peggy Rajski, Maggie Renzi
Director: John Sayles
Screenplay: John Sayles
Cinematography: Ernest R. Dickerson
Editor: John Sayles
Music: Mason Daring
Production Design: Nora Chavooshian
Art Direction: Stephen J. Lineweaver
Cast: Joe Morton (The Brother), Darryl Edwards (Fly), Steve James (Odell), Leonard Jackson (Smokey), Bill Cobbs (Walter), Ren Woods (Bernice), Maggie Renzi (Noreen), Tom Wright (Sam), Caroline Aaron (Randy Sue

Carter), John Sayles (Man in Black), David Strathairn (Man in Black), Jaime Tirelli (Hector), Dee Dee Bridgewater (Malverne Davis), Sidney Sheriff Jr. (Virgil), Edward Baran (Mr. Vance), Josh Mostel (Casio vendor)
Format: 35 mm (1.85 : 1)
108 min.

"Born in the USA," Bruce Springsteen (Music Video, 1984)
Director: John Sayles
Camera: Ernest Dickerson, Michael Ballhaus

"I'm On Fire," Bruce Springsteen (Music Video, 1985)
Director: John Sayles
Camera: Michael Ballhaus

"Glory Days," Bruce Springsteen (Music Video, 1985)
Director: John Sayles
Camera: Michael Ballhaus

Matewan (1987)
Production Companies: Cinecom Entertainment Group, Red Dog Films, Film Gallery, Goldcrest Films International
Distributor: Cinecom Pictures
Executive Producers: Martin Balsam, Amir Jacob Malin, Jerry Silva
Producers: Peggy Rajski, Maggie Renzi
Director: John Sayles
Screenplay: John Sayles
Cinematography: Haskell Wexler
Editor: Sonya Polonsky
Music: Mason Daring
Production Design: Nora Chavooshian
Art Direction: Dan Bishop
Costume Design: Cynthia Flynt
Cast: Chris Cooper (Joe Kenehan), Mary McDonnell (Elma Radnor), Will Oldham (Danny Radnor), David Strathairn (Sid Hatfield), Ken Jenkins (Sephus Purcell), Kevin Tighe (Hickey), Gordon Clapp (Griggs), Bob Gunton (C. E. Lively), Jace Alexander (Hillard Elkins), Joe Grifasi (Fausto), Nancy Mette (Bridey Mae), Jo Henderson (Mrs. Elkins), Josh Mostel (Cabell Testerman), Maggie Renzi (Rosaria), John Sayles (Hardshell Preacher), James Earl Jones (Few Clothes)
Format: 35 mm (1.85 : 1)
135 min.

Eight Men Out (1988)
Production Company: Orion Pictures Corporation
Distributor: Orion Pictures Corporation
Executive Producers: Barbara Boyle, Jerry Offsay

Producers: Sarah Pillsbury, Midge Sanford
Director: John Sayles
Screenplay: John Sayles
Based on the book by: Eliot Asinof
Cinematography: Robert Richardson
Editor: John Tintori
Music: Mason Daring
Production Design: Nora Chavooshian
Art Direction: Dan Bishop
Costume Design: Cynthia Flynt
Cast: John Cusack (George "Buck" Weaver), Clifton James (Charles "Commie" Comiskey), Michael Lerner (Arnold Rothstien), Christopher Lloyd ("Sleepy" Bill Burns), John Mahoney (William Kid Gleason), Charlie Sheen (Oacar "Hap" Felsch), David Strathairn (Eddie Cicotte), D. B. Sweeney (Joseph "Shoeless Joe" Jackson), Michael Rooker (Arnold "Chick" Gandil), Don Harvey (Charles "Swede" Risberg), James Read (Claude "Lefty" Williams), Perry Lang (Fred McMullin), Gordon Clapp (Ray Scalk), Jace Alexander (Dickie Kerr), Bill Irwin (Eddie Collins), Richard Edson (Billy Haharg), Kevin Tighe (Joseph "Sport" Sullivan), Michael Mantell (Abe Attell), John Anderson (Judge Kenesaw Mountain Landis), Studs Terkel (Hugh Fullerton), James Desmond (Smitty), John Sayles (Ring Lardner), Eliot Asinoff (John Heydler), Clyde Bassett (Ben Johnson), Michael Laskin (Alfred Austrian), Barbara Garrick (Helen Weaver), Wendy Makkena (Kate Jackson), Maggie Renzi (Rose Cicotte), Tay Strathairn (Bucky), Jesse Vincent (Scooter)
Format: 35 mm (1.85 : 1)
119 min.

City of Hope (1991)
Production Companies: Esperanza Films Inc., The Samuel Goldwyn Company
Distributor: The Samuel Goldwyn Company
Executive Producers: John Sloss, Harold Webb
Producers: Sarah Green, Maggie Renzi
Director: John Sayles
Screenplay: John Sayles
Cinematography: Robert Richardson
Editor: John Sayles
Music: Mason Daring
Production Design: Dan Bishop, Dianna Freas
Art Direction: Chas Plummer
Costume Design: John A. Dunn
Cast: Vincent Spano (Nick Rinaldi), Stephen Mendillo (Yoyo), Chris Cooper (Riggs), Tony Lo Bianco (Joe Rinaldi), Joe Morton (Wynn), Charlie Yanko

(Stavros), Jace Alexander (Bobby), Todd Graff (Zip), Scott Tiler (Vinnie), John Sayles (Carl), Frankie Faison (Levonne), Gloria Foster (Jeanette), Tom Wright (Malik), Angela Bassett (Reesha), David Strathairn (Asteroid), Maggie Renzi (Connie), Anthony John Denison (Rizzo), Kevin Tighe (O'Brien), Michael Mantell (Zimmer), Josh Mostel (Mad Anthony), Jojo Smollett (Desmond), Edward Jay Townsend Jr. (Tito), Joe Grifasi (Pauly), Louis Zorich (Mayor Baci), Gina Gershon (Laurie Rinaldi), Bill Raymond (Les)
Format: 35 mm Panavision (2.35 : 1)
129 min.

Passion Fish (1992)
Production Company: Archafalaya
Distributor: Miramax Films
Executive Producer: John Sloss
Producers: Sarah Green, Maggie Renzi
Director: John Sayles
Screenplay: John Sayles
Cinematography: Roger Deakins
Editor: John Sayles
Music: Mason Daring
Production Design: Dan Bishop, Dianna Freas
Costume Design: Cynthia Flynt
Cast: Mary McDonnell (May-Alice Culhane), Alfre Woodard (Chantelle), David Strathairn (Rennie), Vondie Curtis-Hall (Sugar LeDoux), Angela Bassett (Rhonda/Dawn), Leo Burmester (Reeves), Tom Wright (Luther), Nancy Mette (Nina), Maggie Renzi (Louise), Lenore Banks (Nurse Quick), Will Mahoney (Max), Michael Laskin (Redwood Vance)
Format: 35 mm (1.85 : 1)
135 min.

The Secret of Roan Inish (1994)
Production Companies: Jones Entertainment Group, Skerry Productions
Distributor: The Samuel Goldwyn Company
Executive Producers: Glenn R. Jones, Peter Newman, John Sloss
Producers: Sarah Green, Maggie Renzi
Director: John Sayles
Screenplay: John Sayles
Based on a book by: Rosalie K. Fry (*The Secret of Ron Mor Skerry*)
Cinematography: Haskell Wexler
Editor: John Sayles
Music: Mason Daring
Production Design: Adrian Smith
Costume Design: Consolata Boyle

Cast: Jeni Courtney (Fiona), Mick Lally (Hugh), Eileen Colgan (Tess), John Lynch (Tadhg), Richard Sheridan (Eamon), Susan Lynch (Selkie), Dave Duffy (Jim), Declan Hannigan (Oldest Brother), Gerard Rooney (Liam), Cillian Byrne (Jamie)
Format: 35 mm (1.85 : 1)
103 min.

Lone Star (1996)
Production Companies: Columbia Pictures Corporation, Castle Rock Entertainment, Rio Dulce
Distributor: Sony Pictures Classics
Executive Producer: John Sloss
Producers: R. Paul Miller, Maggie Renzi
Director: John Sayles
Screenplay: John Sayles
Cinematography: Stuart Dryburgh
Editor: John Sayles
Music: Mason Daring
Production Design: Dan Bishop
Art Direction: J. Kyler Black
Costume Design: Shay Cunliffe
Cast: Chris Cooper (Sam Deeds), Elizabeth Peña (Pilar Cruz), Joe Morton (Delmore "Del" Payne), Kris Kristofferson (Charlie Wade), Matthew McConaughey (Buddy Deeds), Miriam Colon (Mercedes Cruz), Clifton James (Hollis), Jeff Monahan (Young Hollis), Ron Canada (Otis Payne), Gabriel Casseus (Young Otis), Stephen Mendillo (Cliff), Stephen J. Lang (Mikey), LaTanya Richardson (Priscilla Worth), Tony Frank (Fenton), Leo Burmester (Cody), Vanessa Martinez (Young Pilar), Tay Strathairn (Young Sam), Frances McDormand (Bunny)
Format: 35 mm, Super 35 (2.35 : 1)
135 min.

Men with Guns/Hombres Armados (1997)
Production Companies: Anarchist's Convention Films, Clear Blue Sky Productions, Independent Film Channel, Lexington Road Productions
Distributor: Sony Pictures Classics
Executive Producers: Jody Allen, Lou Gonda, John Sloss
Producers: R. Paul Miller, Maggie Renzi
Director: John Sayles
Screenplay: John Sayles
Cinematography: Slawomir Idziak
Editor: John Sayles
Music: Mason Daring
Production Design: Felipe Fernández del Paso

Art Direction: Salvador Parra
Costume Design: Mayes C. Rubeo
Cast: Frederico Luppi (Dr. Fuentes), Damián Delgado (Domingo, the Soldier), Dan Rivera González (Conejo, the Boy), Tania Cruz (Graciela, the Mute Girl), Damián Alcázar (Padre Portillo), Mandy Patinkin (Andrew), Kathryn Grody (Harriet), Iguandili López (Mother), Nandi Luna Ramirez (Daughter) Rafaeil de Quevedo (General), Carmen Madrid (Angela), Esteban Sorberanes (Raúl), Iván Arango (Cienfuegos), Lizzie Curry Martinez (Montoya), Roberto Sosa (Bravo)
Format: 35 mm (1.85 : 1)
127 min.

Limbo (1999)
Production Company: Green/Renzi
Distributor: Screen Gems
Producer: Maggie Renzi
Director: John Sayles
Screenplay: John Sayles
Cinematography: Haskell Wexler
Editor: John Sayles
Music: Mason Daring
Production Design: German Jackson
Art Direction: Keith Neely
Costume Design: Shay Cunliffe
Cast: Mary Elizabeth Mastrantonio (Donna De Angelo), David Strathairn ("Jumpin" Joe Gastineau), Vanessa Martinez (Noelle De Angelo), Kris Kristofferson ("Smilin" Jack Johannson), Casey Siemaszko (Bobby Gastineau), Kathryn Grody (Frankie), Leo Burmester (Harmon King), Michael Laskin (Albright)
Format: 35 mm (1.85 : 1)
126 min.

Sunshine State (2002)
Production Company: Anarchist's Convention
Distributor: Sony Pictures Classics
Producer: Maggie Renzi
Director: John Sayles
Screenplay: John Sayles
Cinematography: Patrick Cady
Editor: John Sayles
Music: Mason Daring
Production Design: Mark Ricker
Art Direction: Shawn Carroll
Costume Design: Mayes C. Rubeo

Cast: Jane Alexander (Delia Temple), Angela Bassett (Desiree Perry), Gordon Clapp (Earl Pinkney), Edie Falco (Marly Temple) Miguel Ferrer (Lester), Timothy Hutton (Jack Meadows), Alan King (Murray Silver), James McDaniel (Reggie Perry), Mary Steenburgen (Francine Pinkney), Bill Cobbs (Dr. Lloyd), Cullen Douglas (Jefferson Cash), Clifton James (Buster Bidwell), Eliot Asinof (Silent Sam), Alex Lewis (Terrell), Tom Wright (Flash Phillips), Richard Edson (Steve Tregaskis)
Format: 35 mm (1:85 : 1)
141 min.

Casa de los babys (2003)
Production Companies: IFC Films, Springall Pictures, Blue Magic Pictures
Distributor: IFC Films
Executive Producers: Caroline Kaplan, Jonathan Sehring
Producers: Alejandro Springall, Lemore Syvan
Director: John Sayles
Screenplay: John Sayles
Cinematography: Mauricio Rubinstein
Editor: John Sayles
Music: Mason Daring
Production Design: Felipe Fernández del Paso
Costume Design: Mayes C. Rubeo
Cast: Vanessa Martinez (Asunción), Rita Moreno (Señora Muñoz), Daryl Hannah (Skipper), Lili Taylor (Leslie), Mary Steenburgen (Gayle), Marcia Gay Harden (Nan), Maggie Gyllenhaal (Jennifer), Susan Lynch (Eileen), Bruno Bichir (Diómedes), Juan Carlos Vives (Búho)
Format: 35 mm (1:85 : 1)
95 min.

Silver City (2004)
Production Company: Anarchist's Convention Films
Distributor: Newmarket Films
Producer: Maggie Renzi
Director: John Sayles
Screenplay: John Sayles
Cinematography: Haskell Wexler
Editor: John Sayles
Music: Mason Daring
Production Design: Toby Corbett
Costume Design: Shay Cunliffe
Cast: Chris Cooper (Dickie Pilager), Richard Dreyfuss (Chuck Raven), Danny Huston (Danny O'Brien), Mary Kay Place (Grace Seymour), Billy Zane (Chandler Tyson), Miguel Ferrer (Cliff Castleton), Michael Murphy (Senator Judson Pilager), Kris Kristofferson (Wes Benteen), Daryl Hannah

(Maddy Pilager), Tim Roth (Mitch Paine), Thora Birch (Karen Cross), Maria Bello (Nora Allardyce), Luis Saguar (Vince Esparza), Sal Lopez (Tony Guerra), James Gammon (Sherriff Joe Skaggs)
Format: 16 mm (1.85 : 1)
128 min.

Honeydripper (2007)
Production Company: Anarchist's Convention Films, Honeydripper Films
Distributor: Emerging Pictures
Producer: Maggie Renzi
Director: John Sayles
Screenplay: John Sayles
Cinematography: Dick Pope
Editor: John Sayles
Music: Mason Daring
Production Design: Toby Corbett
Art Direction: Eloise Crane Stammerjohn
Costume Design: Hope Hanafin
Cast: Danny Glover (Tyrone Purvis), Lisa Gay Hamilton (Delilah), Yaya DaCosta (China Doll), Charles S. Dutton (Maceo), Vondie Curtis-Hall (Slick), Gary Clark Jr. (Sonny), Mable John (Bertha Mae), Stacy Keach (Sheriff), Mary Steenburgen (Amanda Winship), Keb' Mo' (Possum), Tom Wright (Cool Breeze)
Format: 35 mm (1:85 : 1)
124 min.

Amigo (2011)
Production Company: Pinoy Pictures
Distributor: Variance Films
Producer: Maggie Renzi
Director: John Sayles
Screenplay: John Sayles
Cinematography: Lee Meily
Editor: John Sayles
Music: Mason Daring
Production Design: Rodell Cruz
Art Direction: Ann Rey Bajar-Banayad
Costume Design: Gino Gonzales
Cast: Chris Cooper (Col. Hardacre), Garret Dilahunt (Lt. Compton), D. J. Qualls (Zeke), Lucas Neff (Shanker), Yul Vazquez (Padre Hidalgo), Dane De Haan (Gil), Stephen Taylor (Private Bates), Bill Tangradi (Dutch), Joel Torre (Rafael), Irma Adlawan (Josefa)

Bibliography

Adams, Anna. "Forget the Alamo: Thinking about History in John Sayles' *Lone Star*." *The History Teacher* 40.3 (2007): 339–47.

Anderson, John. "Down South, Singing the Indie Blues." *New York Times*, Dec. 2, 2007. http://proquest.umi.com/pqdweb?did=1391772361&sid=1&Fmt=3&clientId=3259&RQT=309&VName=PQD; accessed Sept. 5, 2011.

Ansen, David. "The Goodbye Girl." *Newsweek*, Apr. 11, 1983, 78.

Arreola, Daniel D. "Forget the Alamo: Border As Place in John Sayles' *Lone Star*." *Journal of Cultural Geography* 23.1 (2005): 23–42.

Arriola, Elvia. "*Lone Star* and the Faces of Despair in INS Raids." *The Latino/a Condition: A Critical Reader*, eds. Richard Delgado and Jean Stefancic. New York: NYU Press, 1998, 230–36.

Asinof, Eliot. *Eight Men Out: The Black Sox and the 1919 World Series*. New York: Holt, 1963.

Attanasio, Paul. "Listen to 'Brother.'" *Washington Post*, Nov. 16, 1984, C1.

Bakewell, Geoffrey. "Oedipus Tex: *Lone Star*, Tragedy and Postmodernism." *Classical and Modern Literature* 22.1 (2002): 35–48.

Barol, Bill, et al. "He's On Fire." *Newsweek*, Aug. 5, 1985, 51.

Baron, Cynthia. "Sayles between Systems: Bucking 'Industry Policy' and Indie Apolitical Chic." In Carson and Kenaga, 16–50.

Barr, Alan P. "The Borders of Time, Place, and People in John Sayles's *Lone Star*." *Journal of American Studies* 37.3 (2003): 365–74.

Barthes, Roland. *S/Z*. trans. Richard Miller. New York: Hill and Wang, 1974.

Berrera, Cordelia. "Border Theory, and the Politics of Place, Space, and Memory in John Sayles's *Lone Star*." *Quarterly Review of Film and Video* 27.3 (2010): 210–18.

Biskind, Peter. *Down and Dirty Pictures: Miramax, Sundance, and the Rise of Independent Film*. New York: Simon, 2004.

Bould, Mark. *The Cinema of John Sayles: "Lone Star."* Directors' Cuts. London: Wallflower Press, 2009.

Boyd, Melba. "But Not the Blackness of Space: *The Brother from Another Planet* as Icon from the Underground." *Journal of the Fantastic in the Arts*. 2.2 (2010): 95–107.

Brier, Stephen. "A History Film without Much History." *Radical History Review* 41 (1988): 120–28.
Brooks, Peter. *Realist Vision*. New Haven: Yale University Press, 2005.
Canby, Vincent. Review of *Matewan*. *New York Times*, Aug. 28, 1987. http://www.nytimes.com/1987/08/28/movies/film-john-sayles-s-matewan.html?scp=2&sq=Canby+Matewan&st=nyt; accessed Sept. 20, 2011.
———. "Urban America in Microcosm." *New York Times*, Oct. 11, 1991. http://movies.nytimes.com/movie/review?res=9D0CE7D81E38F932A25753C1A967958260; accessed Sept. 20, 2011.
Carson, Diane. "Plain and Simple: Masculinity through John Sayles's Lens." *More than a Method: Trends and Traditions in Contemporary Film Performance*, eds. Cynthia A. Baron, Diane Carson, and Frank P. Tomasulo. Detroit: Wayne State University Press, 2004, 173–88.
———. "John Sayles, Independent Filmmaker: 'Bet on Yourself.'" *Contemporary American Independent Film: From the Margins to the Mainstream*, eds. Chris Holmlund and Justin Wyatt. London: Routledge, 2005, 125–39.
———, ed. *John Sayles: Interviews*. Jackson: University of Mississippi Press, 1999.
———, and Heidi Kenaga. *Sayles Talk: New Perspectives on Independent Filmmaker John Sayles*. Detroit: Wayne State University Press, 2006.
Clark-Jones, Melissa. "*Lone Star*: Renovation of the American Dream." *Studies in Popular Culture* 20.3 (1998): 57–69.
Corliss, Richard. "Nostalgia at 30." *Time* (Sept. 15, 1980). http://www.time.com/time/magazine/article/0,9171,924476,00.html; accessed Sept. 20, 2011.
———. "Dead End on Sesame Street." *Time* (Oct. 21, 1991). http://www.time.com/time/magazine/article/0,9171,974077,00.html; accessed Sept. 20, 2011.
Davis, Todd F., and Kenneth Womack. "Forget the Alamo: Reading the Ethics of Style in John Sayles's *Lone Star*." *Style* 32.3 (1998): 471–85.
DiCaprio, Lisa. "'*Lianna*' Liberal Lesbianism." *Jump Cut* (Feb. 1984): 45–47.
Dittmar, Linda. "All that Hollywood Allows: Film and the Working Class." *Radical Teacher* 46 (1995): 38–46.
Doane, Mary Ann. *The Desire to Desire: The Woman's Film of the 1940s*. Bloomington: Indiana University Press, 1987.
DuCille, Ann. "The Sterile Cuckoo Racha: Debugging *Lone Star*." *Chicana Feminisms: A Critical Reader*, eds. Gabriela F. Arredondo, Aida Hurtado, Norma Klahn, Olga Najera-Ramirez, and Patricia Zavella. Durham: Duke University Press, 2003, 349–53.
Ebert, Roger. Review of *Silver City*. *Chicago Sun-Times*, Sept. 17, 2004. http://rogerebert.suntimes.com/apps/pbcs.dll/article?AID=/20040917/REVIEWS/409170303/1023; accessed Sept. 20, 2011.
Embry, Marcus. "A Postcolonial Tale of Complicity: The 'Angel of History' and *Men with Guns*." *Discourse* 21.1 (1999): 163–80.
Felleman, Susan. "Oedipus Edits (*Lone Star*)." In Carson and Kenaga, 158–73.

Fishbein, Leslie. "John Sayles' *Matewan* (1987): Violence and Nostalgia." *Film and History* 18.3 (1988): 63–67.

Foner, Eric. "*Matewan*." *Past Imperfect: History according to the Movies*, ed. Mark C. Carnes. New York: Holt, 1995, 204–7.

Fregoso, Rosa Linda. "Imagining Multiculturalism: Race and Sexuality on the Tejas Borderlands." *The Review of Education/Pedagogy/Cultural Studies* 21.2 (1999): 133–48.

———. "Recycling Colonialist Fantasies on the Texas Borderlands." *Home, Exile, Homeland: Film, Media, and the Politics of Place*, ed. Hamid Naficy. New York: Routledge, 1999, 169–92.

———. "Reproduction and Miscegenation on the Borderlands: Mapping the Maternal Body of Tejanas." *Chicana Feminisms: A Critical Reader*, eds. Gabriela F. Arredondo, Aida Hurtado, Norma Klahn, Olga Najera-Ramirez, and Patricia Zavella. Durham: Duke University Press, 2003, 324–48.

French, Philip. Review of *Silver City*. "Body of Evidence." *Observer*, July 24, 2005. http://www.guardian.co.uk/film/2005/jul/24/philipfrench; accessed Sept. 20, 2011.

Frye, Northrop. *The Anatomy of Criticism: Four Essays*. Princeton: Princeton University Press, 1954.

Gaines, Jane. "Women and Representation: Can We Enjoy Alternative Pleasure?" *Issues in Feminist Film Criticism*, ed. Patricia Erens. Bloomington: Indiana University Press, 1990.

Giardiana, Denise. *Storming Heaven*. New York: Norton, 1987.

Gordon, Rebecca M. "Psychic Borders and Legacies in *Lone Star* and *Men with Guns*." In Carson and Kenaga, 215–37.

Handley, George B. "Oedipus in the Americas: *Lone Star* and the Reinvention of American Studies." *Forum for Modern Language Studies* 40.2 (2004): 160–81.

Holden, Stephen. Review of *Casa de los babys*. *New York Times*, Sept. 19, 2003. http://movies.nytimes.com/movie/review?_r=1&res=980CE3DB123AF93AA2575AC0A9659C8B63; accessed Sept. 20, 2011.

Holmlund, Christine. "When Is a Lesbian Not a Lesbian? The Lesbian Continuum and the Mainstream Femme Film." *Camera Obscura* 25–26 (1991): 145–78.

Irwin, John T. *Doubling and Incest, Repetition and Revenge: A Speculative Reading of Faulkner*. Baltimore: Johns Hopkins University Press, 1975.

Isaacs, Neil D. "John Sayles and the Fictional Origin of *Matewan*." *Literature/Film Quarterly* 16.4 (1988): 269–71.

Jameson, Fredric. *Postmodernism, or, the Cultural Logic of Late Capitalism*. Durham: Duke University Press, 1991.

Kaminsky, Amy. "Identity at the Border: Narrative Strategies in Maria Novaro's *El Jardin del Eden* and John Sayles's *Lone Star*." *Studies in 20th Century Literature* 25.1 (2001): 91–117.

Kauffmann, Stanley. "Cruelties." *The New Republic*, Mar. 23, 1998, 24.

Kellman, Steven G. "Sayles Goes Spanish: Is *Hombres Armados* a Foreign Film?" *Hopscotch: A Cultural Review* 1.1 (1999): 24–35.

Kempley, Rita. "Coal-Hearted *Matewan*." *Washington Post*, Oct. 16, 1987, D7.

———. "*Eight Men Out*: A Slow Sinker." *Washington Post*, Sept. 23, 1988, B1.

———. "*City of Hope*." *Washington Post*, Oct. 19, 1991. http://www.washingtonpost.com/wp-srv/style/longterm/movies/videos/cityofhope rkempley_a0a277.htm; accessed Sept. 20, 2011.

Keough, Peter. "Earnest Director Puts Life in *Matewan*." *Chicago Sun-Times*, Sept. 18, 1987. http://www.highbeam.com/doc/1P2-3845864.html; accessed Sept. 20, 2011.

King, Geoff. *American Independent Cinema*. Bloomington: Indiana University Press, 2005.

Kraver, Jeraldine R. "Mining Zola's Naturalism: Creating Coherence in the Coal Pits in Germinal, King Coal, and Matewan." *Excavatio: Emile Zola and Naturalism* 13 (2000): 214–24.

Leen, Catherine. "Three Border Films: *El Mariachi*, *El Jardin del Eden* and *Lone Star*." *Cultura Popular: Studies in Spanish and Latin American Popular Culture* (2001): 97–112.

Limón, José E. "Tex-Sex-Mex: American Identities, Lone Stars, and the Politics of Racialized Sexuality." *National Imaginaries, American Identities: The Cultural Work of American Iconography*, eds. Larry Reynolds and Gordon Hutner. Princeton: Princeton University Press, 2000, 229–45.

Linebaugh, Peter, and Marcus Rediker. *The Many-Headed Hydra: Sailors, Slaves, Commoners, and the Hidden History of the Revolutionary Atlantic*. Boston: Beacon, 2000.

Lukács, Georg. *Studies in European Realism: A Sociological Survey of the Writings of Balzac, Stendhal, Zola, Tolstoy, Gorki, and Others*. London: Hillway, 1950.

———. "Narrate or Describe?" *Realism in Our Time: Literature and the Class Struggle*. New York: Harper, 1964, 110–48.

MacCabe, Colin. "Theory and Film: Principles of Realism and Pleasure." *Tracking the Signifier: Theoretical Essays: Film, Linguistics, Literature*. Minneapolis: University of Minnesota Press, 1985, 58–81.

———. "Realism: Balzac and Barthes." *Tracking the Signifier: Theoretical Essays: Film, Linguistics, Literature*. Minneapolis: University of Minnesota Press, 1985, 131–50.

Magowan, Kim. "Blood Only Means What You Let It." *Film Quarterly* 57.1 (2003): 20–31.

Marney, Angela. "*Lianna*: A Move toward Better Things." *Off Our Backs*, Apr. 30, 1983, 18.

Marx, Karl, and Frederick Engels. *The German Ideology: Part One*. trans. C. J. Arthur. New York: International, 1970.

Maslin, Janet. "Baby, It's You." *New York Times*, Mar. 25, 1983. http://www.nytimes.com/1983/03/25/movies/baby-it-s-you.html; accessed Sept. 20, 2011.

Mendoza, Louis. "Representing Chicanas? The Poetics of History, Desire, and Identity in the Lone Star State." *Journal of the American Studies Association of Texas* 29 (2008): 18–38.
Merck, Mandy. "*Lianna* and the Lesbians of Art Cinema." *Films for Women*, ed. Charlotte Brundson. London: BFI, 1986, 166–75.
Meyer, Carla. "Telling His Own Stories." *San Francisco Chronicle*, June 23, 2002, DAT 31.
Miller, Joshua. "The Transamerican Trail to Cerca del Cielo: John Sayles and the Aesthetics of Multilingual Cinema." *Bilingual Games: Some Literary Investigations*, ed. Doris Somer. New York: Palgrave MacMillan, 2003, 121–45.
Molyneaux, Gerry. *John Sayles: An Unauthorized Biography of the Pioneering Indie Filmmaker*. Los Angeles: Renaissance Books, 2000.
Moore, Marat. "Where the Rubber Meets the Road: John Sayles Talks about His Coal Mining Movie *Matewan*." *Now and Then* 5.1 (Spring1988): 5–8.
Newman, Michael Z. "Character and Complexity in American Independent Cinema: *21 Grams* and *Passion Fish*." *Film Criticism* 31.1–2 (2006): 89–106.
Packer, George. "Decency and Muck: The Visions of John Sayles and Oliver Stone." *Dissent* 44.3 (1997): 105–9.
Pagel, James F., Dennis Crow, and John Sayles. "Filmed Dreams: Cinematographic and Story Line Characteristics of the Cinematic Dreamscapes of John Sayles." *Dreaming* 13.1 (2003): 43–48.
Raab, Josef. "Chicanos and Anglos: Mestizaje in Jovita Gonzalez, Gloria Anzaldua, and John Sayles." *Zeitschrift fur Anglistik und Amerikanistik* 47.4 (1999): 344–56.
Ray, Robert B. *A Certain Tendency of the Hollywood Cinema, 1930–1980*. Princeton: Princeton University Press, 1985.
Rizzo, Cindy. "Love and Learn: *Lianna*." *Gay Community News*, Feb. 19, 1983, 7.
Roberts, Nora. "John Sayles and the Un 'Disappearance' of the Working Class: The Vitality of Our History." *Against the Current* 12.4 (1997): 39–42.
Ross, Bob. "Sayles Basks in Sunshine." *Tampa Tribune*, Aug. 2, 2002, 20.
Ryan, Jack. *John Sayles, Filmmaker: A Critical Study and Filmography*, 2nd ed. Jefferson, N.C.: McFarland, 2010.
Sarris, Andrew. "Sayles' Compelling Characters Get Mired in His Despair." *New York Observer*, June 6, 1999. http://www.observer.com/1999/06/sayles-compelling-characters-get-mired-in-his-despair/; accessed Sept. 20, 2011.
Savage, Lon. *Thunder in the Mountains: The West Virginia Mine War 1920–21*. Pittsburgh: University of Pittsburgh Press, 1990.
Sayles, John. *Union Dues*. Boston: Little, Brown, 1977.
———. Foreword. *Thunder in the Mountains: The West Virginia Mine War 1920–21*. Pittsburgh: University of Pittsburgh Press, 1990, vii–viii.
———. *Los Gusanos*. New York: HarperCollins, 1991.
———. Introduction. *"Men with Guns" and "Lone Star."* London: Faber, 1998, vii–x.

———. *Thinking in Pictures: The Making of the Movie "Matewan."* New York: Da Capo, 2003 [1987].

———. Introduction. *"Passion Fish," "Silver City" and Other Screen Plays.* New York: Nation, 2004, 321–22.

Scott, Jay. "Brother's Reach Exceeds Grasp." *Globe and Mail*, Oct. 13, 1984.

Selby, Emily F., and Deborah P. Dixon. "Between Worlds: Considering Celtic Feminine Identities in *The Secret of Roan Inish*." *Gender, Place and Culture* 5.1 (1998): 5–24.

Shumway, David R. *Modern Love: Romance, Intimacy, and the Marriage Crisis*. New York: NYU Press, 2003.

Sloterdijk, Peter. *Critique of Cynical Reason*. trans. Michael Eldred. Minneapolis: University of Minnesota Press, 1987.

Smith, Gavin, ed., and John Sayles. *Sayles on Sayles.* London: Faber and Faber, 1998.

Somerson, Wendy. "White Men on the Edge: Rewriting the Borderlands in *Lone Star*." *Men and Masculinities* 6.3 (2004): 215–39.

Stacey, Jackie. "If You Don't Play, You Can't Win: *Desert Hearts* and the Lesbian Romance Film." *Immortal Invisible: Lesbians and the Moving Image*, ed. Tamsin Wilson. London: Routledge, 1995.

Starr, Juliana. "Coal Miners' Daughters: Representations of Women in Germinal, Matewan and Harlan County, USA." *Excavatio: Emile Zola and Naturalism* 22.1–2 (2007): 73–86.

Straayer, Chris. *Deviant Eyes, Deviant Bodies: Sexual Re-Orientation in Film and Video*. New York: Columbia University Press, 1996.

Suárez, Juan A. *Jim Jarmusch*. Contemporary Film Directors. Urbana: University of Illinois Press, 2007.

Subramanian, Janani. "Alienating Identification: Black Identity in *The Brother from Another Planet* and *I Am Legend*." *Science Fiction Film and Television* 3.1 (2010): 37–56.

Sugg, Katherine. "Multicultural Masculinities and the Border Romance in John Sayles's *Lone Star* and Cormac McCarthy's *Border Trilogy*." *The New Centennial Review* 1.3 (2001): 117–54.

Sultze, Kimberly. "Rewriting the West as Multi-Cultural: Legend Meets Complex Histories in la Frontera in John Sayles' *Lone Star*." *Film and History* 33.2 (2003): 19–25.

———. "Challenging Legends, Complicating Border Lines: The Concept of 'Frontera' in John Sayles's *Lone Star*." *Hollywood's West: The American Frontier in Film, Television, and History*, eds. Peter C. Rollins and John E. O'Connor. Lexington: The University Press of Kentucky, 2005. 261–80.

Thompson, Cliff. "The Brother from Another Race: Black Characters in the Films of John Sayles." *Cineaste* 22.3 (1996): 32–33.

Tormey, Warren. "'You Don't Play the Angles, You're a Sap': John Sayles, Eliot Asinof, Baseball, Labor, and Chicago in 1919." *Baseball/Literature/Culture: Essays*, ed. Peter Carino. Jefferson, N.C.: McFarland, 2004, 60–75.

Tudor, Andy. "*Lone Star.*" *New Humanist* 120.1 (2005): 29.
Turmin, Maureen, and Mika Turmin-Nygren. "Of Spectral Mothers and Lost Children: War, Folklore, and Psychoanalysis in *The Secret of Roan Inish.*" In Carson and Kenaga, 134–57.
Tzioumakis, Yannis. *American Independent Cinema: An Introduction*. New Brunswick: Rutgers University Press, 2006.
Updike, John. "Howells As Anti-Novelist." *Odd Jobs*. New York: Knopf, 1991, 168–89.
Whitehouse, Glenn. "Remember to Forget the Alamo: The Dynamics of Cultural Memory in John Sayles' *Lone Star.*" *Literature and Theology* 16.3 (2002): 291–310.
Williams, Joe. "A Call from Sayles Is a Reminder to Heed the Movie Mavericks." *St. Louis Post-Dispatch*, Oct 10, 2003, E.1. http://proquest.umi.com/pqdweb?did=422409551&Fmt=3&clientId=3259&RQT=309&VName=PQD; accessed Sept. 20, 2011.
Williams, John A. "John Sayles Plays the Preacher." *Appalachian Journal* 15.4 (1988): 344–52.
Žižek, Slovoj. *The Sublime Object of Ideology*. London: Verso, 1989.

Index

Page numbers in italics refer to illustrations; page numbers in bold refer to overview sections for particular film titles.

David R. Shumway is the director of the Humanities Center and a professor of English and literary and cultural studies at Carnegie Mellon University. His many books include *Modern Love: Romance, Intimacy, and the Marriage Crisis.*

Books in the series
Contemporary Film Directors

Nelson Pereira dos Santos
Darlene J. Sadlier

Abbas Kiarostami
Mehrnaz Saeed-Vafa and Jonathan Rosenbaum

Joel and Ethan Coen
R. Barton Palmer

Claire Denis
Judith Mayne

Wong Kar-wai
Peter Brunette

Edward Yang
John Anderson

Pedro Almodóvar
Marvin D'Lugo

Chris Marker
Nora Alter

Abel Ferrara
Nicole Brenez, translated by Adrian Martin

Jane Campion
Kathleen McHugh

Jim Jarmusch
Juan Suárez

Roman Polanski
James Morrison

Manoel de Oliveira
John Randal Johnson

Neil Jordan
Maria Pramaggiore

Paul Schrader
George Kouvaros

Jean-Pierre Jeunet
Elizabeth Ezra

Terrence Malick
Lloyd Michaels

Sally Potter
Catherine Fowler

Atom Egoyan
Emma Wilson

Albert Maysles
Joe McElhaney

Jerry Lewis
Chris Fujiwara

Jean-Pierre and Luc Dardenne
Joseph Mai

Michael Haneke
Peter Brunette

Alejandro González Iñárritu
Celestino Deleyto and Maria del Mar Azcona

Lars von Trier
Linda Badley

Hal Hartley
Mark L. Berrettini

François Ozon
Thibaut Schilt

Steven Soderbergh
Aaron Baker

Mike Leigh
Sean O'Sullivan

D. A. Pennebaker
Keith Beattie

Jacques Rivette
Mary M. Wiles

Kim Ki-duk
Hye Seung Chung

Philip Kaufman
Annette Insdorf

Richard Linklater
David T. Johnson

David Lynch
Justus Nieland

John Sayles
David R. Shumway

The University of Illinois Press
is a founding member of the
Association of American University Presses.

Designed by Paula Newcomb
Composed in 10/13 New Caledonia LT Std Regular
with Helvetica Neue LT Std display
by Barbara Evans
at the University of Illinois Press
Manufactured by Sheridan Books, Inc.

University of Illinois Press
1325 South Oak Street
Champaign, IL 61820-6903
www.press.uillinois.edu